Entrepreneur MAGAZINE'S

startup

2ND EDITION

'Start Your Own

SEMINAR PRODUCTION BUSINESS

Your Step-by-Step Guide to Success

Entrepreneur Press and Terry, 1952 and Rob Adams

EP
Entrepreneur.
Press

Editorial Director: Jere L. Calmes
Managing Editor: Marla Markman
Cover Design: Beth Hansen-Winter
Production and Composition: Eliot House Productions

This publication is designed to provide accurate and authoritative information in regard
to the subject matter covered. It is sold with the understanding that the publisher is not
engaged in rendering legal, accounting or other professional services. If legal advice or
other expert assistance is required, the services of a competent professional person
should be sought.

Library of Congress Cataloging-in-Publication Data

Adams, Terry, 1952–
   Start your own seminar production business/by Terry and Rob Adams.—2nd ed.
      p.   cm.
   Includes index.
   ISBN 1-59918-036-7 (alk. paper)
      1. Forums (Discussion and debate)—Planning. 2. Forums (Discussion and debate)—
Marketing. 3. Meetings—Planning. 4. Meetings—Marketing. I. Adams, Rob, 1950— II.
Title.
LC6519.A35 2006
374.13'7—dc22   2006021893

Printed in Canada

12 11 10 09 08 07 06   10 9 8 7 6 5 4 3 2 1

Start Your Own

SEMINAR PRODUCTION BUSINESS

Additional titles in *Entrepreneur's **Startup Series***

Start Your Own

Bar and Tavern

Bed & Breakfast

Business on eBay

Business Support Service

Car Wash

Child Care Service

Cleaning Service

Clothing Store

Coin-Operated Laundry

Consulting

Crafts Business

e-Business

e-Learning Business

Event Planning Business

Executive Recruiting Service

Freight Brokerage Business

Gift Basket Service

Growing and Selling Herbs and Herbal
   Products

Home Inspection Service

Import/Export Business

Information Consultant Business

Law Practice

Lawn Care Business

Mail Order Business

Medical Claims Billing Service

Personal Concierge Service

Personal Training Business

Pet-Sitting Business

Restaurant and Five Other Food Businesses

Self-Publishing Business

Specialty Travel & Tour Business

Staffing Service

Successful Retail Business

Vending Business

Wedding Consultant Business

Wholesale Distribution Business

Contents

Chapter 8
Command Center:
Your Business Location

Chapter 9
Your Stage Crew:
Finding and Hiring Speakers and Staff

Chapter 10

Marquee Magic, Part 1:
Direct-Mail Advertising

Chapter 11

Marquee Magic, Part 2:
Promo Kits and Media Time

Chapter 12

The Check's in the Mail:
Effectively Controlling Your Finances

Preface

You're holding this book, either in your hands, on your lap, or on your desk—probably dangerously near a spillable cup of coffee—because you're one of those people who like to live on the edge. You're contemplating starting your own business.

This is one of the most exhilarating things you can do for yourself and your family. It's also one of the scariest.

Owning your own business means you're the boss, the big cheese, the head honcho. You make the rules. You lay down the law. It also means you can't call in sick (especially when you're the only employee), you can't let somebody else worry about making enough to cover payroll and expenses, and you can't defer that cranky client to a higher authority. You're it.

We're assuming you've picked up this book on starting a seminar business for one or more of the following reasons:

- You have a background in the seminar field.
- You're a seminar junkie. Every time one is advertised you want to be front-row center in the audience, and you think the seminar business is fun and exciting.
- You have a background in speaking or training and like helping people learn.
- You have no experience with speaking or training but believe you have a message worth delivering and feel you can deliver it in an entertaining, informative fashion.
- You believe the seminar industry is an up-and-coming one, and you're willing to take a chance.

Which did you choose? (Didn't know it was a test, did you?)

Well, you can relax because there is no wrong answer. Any of these responses is entirely correct so long as you realize that they all involve a lot of learning and a lot of hard work. They can also involve a lot of fun, as well as a tremendous amount of personal and professional satisfaction.

Our goal here is to tell you everything you need to know to decide whether a seminar business is the right business for you, and then, assuming it is, to:

- get your business started successfully,
- keep your business running successfully, and
- make friends and influence people. (That's actually part of Chapters 10 and 11, which are about advertising and public relations.)

We've attempted to make this book as user-friendly as possible. We've interviewed lots of people out there on the front lines of the industry to find out how the seminar business really works. And we've set aside lots of places for them to tell their own stories and give their own hard-won advice and suggestions, a sort of virtual round-table discussion group, with you placed right in the thick of things. (For a listing of these successful business owners, see this book's Appendix.) We've broken our chapters into manageable sections on every aspect of start-up and operations. And we've left some space for your creativity to soar.

We've packed our pages with helpful tips so that you can get up and running on your new venture as quickly as possible. And we have provided an Appendix crammed with contacts and sources.

So sit back and relax—don't spill that coffee—get reading, and get ready to become a seminar pro.

Seminar Production
Pizazz

The seminar business is big these days, in demand by individual consumers, organizations, associations, small businesses, and giant corporations alike. And although it's a fairly young industry, having really come into its own within the last two decades, it's primed for continued growth and success.

This chapter explores the flourishing seminar business—a sort of in-your-lap TV news magazine report without the commercials. We'll delve into the steadily rising economic success of the field, dip into its secrets and—unlike any TV news magazine—help you decide whether it's the business for you!

Empowered and Enriched

We inhabit a hectic, harried, fast-paced world where just about everybody feels that they are overworked and underaccomplished. Whether you are a busy executive juggling a dozen projects, a salesperson trying to land a dozen accounts, or a stay-at-home parent racing in a dozen different kid-related directions, you feel you could and should be doing more, and doing it better. The buzzwords of the day are empowerment, enrichment, and fulfillment, both personal and professional. And everybody wants to be empowered, enriched, and fulfilled. Which is good. It makes for a society striving for success.

It also makes a healthy market for the seminar professional. Every year, hundreds of thousands of people pay to attend meetings, seminars, workshops and training programs where professional presenters encourage, enlighten, and enliven them. Some of these folks are sent by their companies to learn new skills—everything from time management to basic math smarts to super sales techniques. Others attend on their own, seeking personal growth—how to communicate better with spouses, significant others and kids; manage stress; assert themselves; or invest for the future. Still others sign up for seminars and workshops as part of a professional or social association to learn everything from quilting to romance writing to tax preparation.

"There's a future in the seminar industry for any entrepreneur with a timely topic in which people have a perceived need or in which you can create a need," says Mark Sanborn, president of the National Speakers Association in Tempe, Arizona. But, he asserts, "Audiences don't need more information; they need insights." A good seminar professional is really an information broker who delivers information that audiences can use to enrich their lives.

The Lingo

Which brings us to a good question: What's the difference between a speaker, a presenter and a trainer? Like the varied terminology for seminars themselves, the lingo for seminar-givers is basically a matter of semantics. One person can fill a number of roles, depending on what is being asked of him or her and what the customer or client has in mind. Here's the cheat-sheet version:

- A *speaker* gives talks or speeches before an audience, which is usually (and hopefully) composed of 50 to several thousand people.

- A *trainer* teaches small groups of people specific skills like how to sell more real estate or pass a contractor's license exam or interface on the internet.
- A *presenter* is a sort of all-purpose word for the person who presents or gives a speech, training session or other seminar.
- A *facilitator* (a buzzword of the business) helps or facilitates people to learn intangible things like self-confidence, motivation or creativity.

Stat Fact
The National Speakers Association, an international organization for professional speakers, counts more than 4,000 members in 23 countries.

We're going to use these terms interchangeably, just as we're going to equally use the terms attendees, audience, and participants. Naturally, an audience at a keynote speech is not going to be role-playing or doing those "catch your partner as he falls to demonstrate trust" exercises that were so popular in the consciousness-raising '70s (and still are in some circles). But in most seminars today, there's a fair measure of give-and-take between the attendees and the presenter, so it's smart to think of the people who'll pay your enrollment fees as participants rather than mere seat-fillers.

Semantics Central

There are more types of functions in the seminar business than just seminars—you'll hear people bandying about terms like meetings, workshops, conferences, and training programs. So what's the difference?

Not a whole lot—it's basically a matter of semantics, but to give you an idea of what's what, take a look at the following:

- A *seminar* is a program, which can last from a few hours to a few days, designed to give attendees information on a particular topic, like making winning sales calls.
- A *workshop* is a seminar with a twist—attendees become participants instead of merely an audience through role-playing, quizzes, hands-on demonstrations, and other do-and-learn activities.
- A *training program* is usually the same thing as a workshop: a learning session with attendees participating to some degree in the action.
- *Conferences*, *conventions*, and *meetings* are group get-togethers—also lasting for various time periods, usually over the course of a few days to a week—designed by associations, organizations, corporations, or other groups for their members, and can incorporate all sorts of outsourced speeches, seminars, and workshops.
- A *speech* or *talk* is just what it sounds like—the speaker pontificating before a group of attendees with little or no audience participation—and generally will last anywhere from 30 minutes to two hours.

Choices, Choices

As a seminar professional, you can choose from among three different operating modes. You can:

1. act as a speaker, trainer or presenter, working directly with your audiences and booking your programs on your own or through a speakers bureau (which is sort of like a talent agency),

2. act as a promoter, seminar company or training firm, setting up programs and engaging other people to do the speaking, training, or presenting, or

3. do both, setting up programs at which you present and at which you also bring others on board to share the speaking or training chores.

Most seminar professionals choose the first option, but you can go with any one that feels comfortable to you. We'll discuss all three through the course of this book.

- A *keynote speech* is one that's the highlight of a conference or convention, like a before- or after-dinner speech, a speech that opens the get-together or the grand finale that closes it.

In this book, we're going to use the terms *seminar, workshop,* and *program* more or less interchangeably.

Seminar Customers

Who attends seminars? All sorts of people who hope to gain all sorts of insights.

Businesses are big customers on the seminar scene. Large corporations, having gone through the economic and emotional trauma of downsizing, often decide that hiring out training and motivational seminars is more cost-effective than developing them inhouse. Sometimes they send their employees off-site to attend these events; sometimes they invite the seminar presenter into their own facilities. Smaller companies are good seminar customers for similar reasons. They don't have the inhouse means to

Stat Fact
According to "What Things Cost," a recent article in *T+D* magazine (a publication of the American Society for Training and Development), the fee for development or delivery of customized training can range from $2,000 to $3,000 per day.

develop training and motivational programs, so they rely on outside sources.

This is a hot new field and growing hotter. Outsourced training expenditures rose in a recent six-year period from $9.9 billion to $19.3 billion annually. Popular training topics include customer service and creative problem solving, but they can also encompass internal communications and even math or reading 101. Leadership, self-motivation, and sales motivation are also perennially popular topics.

Professional, civic, and social associations are always on the lookout for keynote speakers to set off their annual conventions as well as to conduct workshops and conferences. Business networking groups are prime candidates for programs on motivation, time management, organization, positive thinking, and goal achievement. Medical societies want to hear about insurance issues, new surgical techniques, and office management.

Seminar Speak

A concurrent or breakout session has nothing to do with breaking out—of prison or in zits—but refers to a seminar or workshop held at the same time as several other seminars or workshops during a convention. Participants can choose which session to attend—for instance, a program on fingerprinting techniques or one on DNA sampling.

Antique Roses and Astrology

Writers' groups are interested in the nitty-gritty of creative thinking and publishing success. New Age groups are terrific consumers of programs on alternative health, astrological predictions, and other metaphysical topics, church groups go for programs

Back of the Room

Seminar professionals generate income by doing more than just giving speeches and supervising workshops. They also earn tidy sums of money from back-of-the-room sales. These are all the peripheral goodies that participants can buy to take home with them. Rock concert promoters display T-shirts, posters and souvenir programs for enthusiastic audience members to snap up. And savvy seminar professionals display books, audiotapes, and videos relating to the program, seminar transcripts, and even—especially in the case of motivational programs—buzzword-emblazoned products like bookmarks, calendars, and yes, even T-shirts.

geared toward incorporating the Bible into their daily lives, and garden clubs thrive on seminars on growing antique roses and successful herb planting.

Beyond all these specialized areas of interest, the public at large is also a terrific seminar consumer. People are anxious to learn how to create quality time with family, find the perfect mate, grow the perfect marriage and the smartest/happiest/best-balanced children, lose weight, gain income, invest wisely, live without fear, and retire comfortably.

There's no shortage of topics for the savvy seminar professional, and there's ample room for growth. We'll explore in depth how to decide which specific subjects are best for you and your company as we go through this book. For now, let's look at an important concept for the smart seminar production professional: generating return business.

Momentum and Money

While most of us have attended at least a couple of seminars that were notable chiefly as powerful sleep-inducers, the goal for a winning program is to enthuse and excite the audience. Seminar production professionals strive for sessions that leave people feeling that:

- they've learned tremendous lessons they can immediately apply to their own situations,
- they can't wait to sign up for another one, and
- they must convince everybody they know to rush out and sign up for the same thing.

The Love Boat

If you like to travel, you're considering the right career—most seminar professionals travel extensively. "Last year I was in Georgia for a month," says Nance Cheifetz of Sense of Delight, who lives in Northern California. "I was in Puerto Rico, on an Alaskan cruise, and in Florida three times."

Gail Hahn of Fun*cilitators recently traveled from her home in Virginia to Africa and India. "That was my goal when I started the business," she says, "to travel the world and see friends and family and explore." Like Cheifetz, Hahn has done programs on cruise ships—and had a ball. "I'm considered a life enrichment speaker," she explains. "I do a few sessions of 30 or 40 minutes each, and the rest of the cruise I play." And she does it in style. "Last time we had a deluxe ocean view," she says. "I started in November, did one in January, and we've got one planned for August. They want me to do more, but it's hard to be gone for that long."

Why? Because a seminar is not a one-shot deal. Although most seminars are traveling productions, moving from city to city over the course of the year, you'll want repeat business to keep the momentum going and the money flowing. People who come away from your programs with a sense of excitement will be eager to sign up the next time you come to town and will actually help sell your sessions.

As a promoter of seminars for businesspeople, you want your attendees to rush back to their offices and give their colleagues glowing reports so that those colleagues will insist the company send them to the next session. If your seminar is geared toward associations, you want them to invite you back next year (and the following year) and to recommend you to other chapters around the country. And if your program is targeted at the general public, your goal is to have your audience enthusing to their friends and family so that they all show up for your next program.

Ziegfeld to King

Now you know the basics of seminars: what they are, who attends them, and how they generate income. But what exactly, we hear you asking, does a seminar production professional do? Good question.

As we've said, most seminar professionals act as a sort of impresario like Florenz Ziegfeld (or Don King), designing the seminar, locating and signing up talented speakers, and then making all the arrangements to provide the audience with a memorable experience—choosing the cities on the tour, making hotel and dining reservations, advertising and marketing the event, selling tickets, and handling back-of-the-room sales.

Most seminar professionals act as their own talent—which makes it easy to locate and sign up the speaker—while others prefer to remain behind the scenes. If you're one of the latter—your knees quake at the thought of going before an audience and you've got the on-stage charisma of Barney Fife—not to worry. There are hundreds of speakers bureaus all over the country that can provide specialized talent for every sort of program. These bureaus function much like Hollywood agents, matching speakers with seminars and taking commissions on successful placements. And since the speaker, not the person who hires him, pays the commission, this is a smart way to go.

Stat Fact

According to a recent survey, the National Speakers Association says its surveyed members' annual total gross revenues from speaking, product sales, and related services ranged from $25,000 or less to more than $1 million. Of the roughly 86 percent who responded, the majority (17.5 percent) counted themselves in the $25,000 and under category; 15.1 percent said they earned $26,000 to $50,000; and 14.5 percent claimed earnings of $51,000 to $75,000.

Crank-Up Costs

One of the Catch-22s of being in business for yourself is that you need money to make money—in other words, you need start-up funds. For the seminar business, these costs range from $5,000 to $25,000. You can start out homebased, which means you won't need to worry about leasing office space. Depending on how you choose to run your company, you may not need employees—at least not for starters.

Your major outlays will be for a computer, software, a printer, a fax machine, and internet access. That leaves advertising and—if you choose to carry them—back-of-the-room, or extra-income, products as your other initial expenses.

Smart Tip

Companies that reward employees with trips to Hawaii, Myrtle Beach golf packages, or family fun tours to Disney World have begun to insist on attendance at some sort of concurrent training program so the whole thing can be written off as a learning expense. This is a good thing for the seminar professional!

Sounds good, and it is, except that direct-mail advertising—the best kind to do in this business—can carry a hefty price tag. Which is not to say your start-up costs will be astronomical. You can start with a limited investment, but you'll have to go heavy on the creativity, and you'll have to try even harder than the next guy or gal to focus your energies on your specific target market. (We'll explore these topics later in this book.)

The Rock of Gibraltar

Besides profits and start-up costs, two other important aspects to consider are risk and stability. You want a business that, like the Rock of Gibraltar, is here to stay. In the seminar world, the stability factors are as strong as you are. People are always on the lookout for ways to enrich their personal, business, and economic lives. If you can design a program that fulfills one of these needs and generates the enthusiasm to keep it going or follow up with a similar program aimed at the same audience, then you've got a winning ticket to a successful business.

Stat Fact

There is longevity in the seminar profession: The National Speakers Association says 34.7 percent of its surveyed members have been speaking for 11 to 20 years.

The risk factor is moderate—less than opening a tofu taco restaurant but more than selling 10-cent coffees to caffeine-deprived commuters. The reason is that, although there's a strong market for both personal and corporate training and development programs of all kinds, you must be able to come up with the magic mix of factors—your customers' wants and needs matched with riveting programs promoted with top-notch marketing skills. If you don't have the

Counting Your Coconuts

What can you expect to make as a seminar professional? The amount's up to you, depending only on how serious you are and how hard you want to work. One of the entrepreneurs we interviewed for this book brings in annual gross revenues of up to $300,000; another's company brings in $120 million. Average annual gross revenues for the industry range from $50,000 to $200,000.

"The business can be very lucrative," Gail Hahn of Reston, Virginia-based Fun*cilitators advises, "depending on how good you are on the platform to entertain, motivate, inspire, and market yourself to the right clients. It can bring in up to seven figures if you're very good—and certainly in the six figures."

As a newbie, you shouldn't expect to earn big bucks immediately. "Test-drive your talent and your topic area of expertise while you still have your day job," Hahn says, "to ensure there is a market for your message and cash flow in your bank account."

Get everything you can going for you at the start. You knew that—it's why you bought this book! Its pages will guide you through every stage of starting your seminar company. But keep in mind that researching the points that pertain to the specific type of business you want to run—and then following through—will be up to you.

right mix, you'll have a hard time making it. Not to worry, though. There's a method to finding that magic mix, and we'll show you how in Chapter 2.

The Right Stuff

OK, you've decided that running a seminar business is potentially profitable. You're willing to invest not only the money but also the time to learn the ropes and become established as a pro. What else should you consider? Personality.

Not everybody is cut out to be a seminar production professional. This is not, for example, a career for the creativity-challenged. It takes lots of foresight to figure out what will be a winning program, to design and construct it so it sells, and to promote it effectively. If you're one of those folks who'd rather undergo a root canal than have to come up with peppy advertising copy, then you don't want to be in the seminar business.

This is also not a career for the time-management deficient. Seminars must be planned and organized months in advance, with everything from the topic and speaker to the dining reservations nailed down early on. If you're a star procrastinator who can't seem to get started on anything until the eleventh hour, then you should definitely look elsewhere for entrepreneurial satisfaction.

And if you plan on presenting your own programs, this is not—obviously—a career for the terminally shy or the terminally boring. You must be able to keep an audience interested and entertained for the length of your seminar and beyond. This doesn't mean you need to be

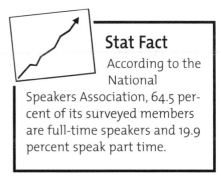

Stat Fact
According to the National Speakers Association, 64.5 percent of its surveyed members are full-time speakers and 19.9 percent speak part time.

trained by both the Royal Shakespeare Academy and the Ringling Brothers Circus school, just that you have a natural enthusiasm for your subjects and be able to communicate it. If you can't do this, then you need to find another option for career success.

But if you delight in dreaming up sparkling programs and star-spangled advertising ideas, you're an efficient time manager and organizer and a pro at helping other people learn, then this is the career for you. The self-evaluation on page 14 will tell you if you have what it takes to become a seminar production pro.

Alternative Careers

This doesn't mean that only ad agency executives or pocket-protector-bearing efficiency experts need apply. Seminar professionals come from all avenues of life. The ones we interviewed for this book encompassed a variety of alternative careers: clinical psychologist, electrical contractor, recreation professional, physician, and sales and marketing professional.

The tip here is that all these entrepreneurs figured out how to make their backgrounds and their interests work for them in their new careers. They've taken the skills and enthusiasm they've already acquired and applied them to the seminar business.

Paid to Play

Gail Hahn turned her knowledge of how to have fun into a successful seminar business, Fun*cilitators. "I've been a recreation professional for over 20 years," she says, "getting paid to play and energize people's lives and help them attain self-actualization through leisure education. From 1986 to 1996, I was the outdoor recreation director in Germany for the Department of Defense. We ran a tennis center, a ropes course, a rental center, and trips throughout Europe and Asia for soldiers and civilians connected with the military.

"Coming back to America in 1996 after blowing out my knee skiing," the Reston, Virginia, resident explains, "I had several months to think about the business plan and my escape from the federal service. I had been planning and plotting for about two years prior with a mastermind group/success team while in Germany. I built my house with a home office to urge me to get the business going and then started the business in January 1997. I kept my day job for about a year and a half to keep the cash flow going.

"The more I got into it, the more committed I became, and the more I found that there was indeed a market of really stressed-out people who needed to be shown how to practice safe stress and mix effectiveness with fun—to get energized and learn how to become playful professionals in order to balance their lives—especially around the DC area."

An Electric Experience

Larry Smith has more than 30 years of experience in the electrical industry, including stints as a master electrician, state electrical inspector, and fire and accident investigator. So doing electrical code training seminars came naturally to him. "I've actually taught seminars part time since 1978," the Omaha, Nebraska, resident says, "but it was plain that there was no market at that time. The market was really created in 1991 through 1993 with the emphasis on training." In 1993, Smith realized he was ready for a change, so he took his company, National Electrical Seminars, full time.

Vintage People

Dr. Jerry Old, a physician and professor at the University of Kansas Medical Center in Kansas City, Kansas, developed his seminar business through his profession, too, but with a twist. Dr. Old began public speaking five years ago on a part-time basis, when he also had a thriving full-time job practicing medicine in the small town of Arkansas City, Kansas. "My interest started in a Toastmasters club and later in formal speech training by a professional trainer," Old says. "A conference put on by [a renowned public speaker] inspired me to pursue this passion of speaking.

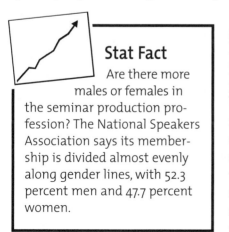

Stat Fact

Are there more males or females in the seminar production profession? The National Speakers Association says its membership is divided almost evenly along gender lines, with 52.3 percent men and 47.7 percent women.

"At the same time, my medical practice was growing older with me—I was 50, but I had a lot of very active 70-, 80-, and 90-year-old patients. I became fascinated with the accomplishments of many of my older patients. I began to study what these people were doing right to live long, healthy, happy lives. The fascinating secrets I have learned from these successful people made me want to share them with others." And that desire to share the secrets to longevity led the doctor to his develop seminars for older Americans or, as he calls them, "Vintage People."

Psychology of Success

Denise Dudley, who lives in the San Luis Obispo, California, area, has been in the seminar business for 15 years. In her "former" life, she was a clinical psychologist and the clinical director for a group of psychiatric hospitals. As the hospitals' director, Dudley found herself doing lots of public speaking and training—everything from talks on mental health and women's issues for local groups to all the training for physicians coming into the hospital.

When Dudley took a sabbatical, she decided to give the seminar business a go, based on her enjoyment of public speaking. She signed on with a national training company and moved from San Francisco to Kansas City—just in time to see the firm go through a major—and extremely unpleasant—partnership shakeup.

"You can't tell the bad news from the good when you're experiencing it," Dudley says philosophically. And with excellent reason, because from that shakeup her own company was born. She and her husband, Jerry, who had been on board the original firm before the shakeup, literally walked across the street and opened their own seminar company, SkillPath Seminars. SkillPath, which is based in Mission, Kansas, gives both public and private seminars on a host of business, professional, and IT topics including business writing and advertising, project and time management, and web site development and security.

"Jerry was the marketing expert," the never-looked-back former psychologist explains, "and I was the curriculum expert." Denise and Jerry decided at the outset to grow SkillPath large, and they succeeded—so well, in fact, that four years ago they sold the company and retired in style to raise their children in the country.

Today SkillPath does 3,000 seminars a month in five countries, with the combined efforts of a 300-person-strong administrative staff and 358 trainers. Sadly, Jerry passed away in 2002, but Denise remains on the board of directors of the firm that is still, as she says, their first baby.

Sense of Delight

In Novato, California, in the San Francisco Bay area, Nance Cheifetz runs a very different company, Sense of Delight. With a master's degree in expressive therapy and a background in sales and marketing, Cheifetz knew she had terrific skills but didn't want to do traditional teaching or work in an institution. So seven years ago, she sat down with a mentor and decided to marry her skills with the marketplace. She realized that everything she did was accomplished with fun, delight, and humor, and hit on doing workshops on creative ways to make life more fun. At first Cheifetz gave seminars on topics like delighting your lover and cooking up adventures on a shoestring.

But when the dotcom crash sent the Bay area's economy crashing along with it, Cheifetz had to reinvent her company. Sense of Delight now specializes in corporate team-building and employee recognition with programs that take old-fashioned sit-down seminars and workshops and transform them into treasure hunts, fishing contests

Now Speaking . . .

If you're going to be a seminar professional, you should know about the National Speakers Association (NSA). The NSA calls itself "the voice of the speaking profession." Its members include experts who are trainers, educators, humorists, motivators, consultants, and authors. Speakers bring their own expertise, and the NSA helps them build business skills and platform performance (which means presenting skills).

Not just any old body can belong to the NSA. To qualify for new membership, you must have made 20 paid presentations, given presentations to an audience of 15 or more as part of a salaried position within the past 12 months, or have received $25,000 in speaking fees in the 12 months prior to your application to the association. (If you don't yet meet one of these qualifications, you can still participate in most of the NSA's programs at nonmember rates.) The perks include:

○ national conventions
○ single-focus labs
○ PEG (Professional Experts Group) conventions, workshops and networking for 12 different specialties including humor, education, health and wellness, sales training, seminars and workshops, and writing and publishing
○ a listing in the NSA's membership directory, *Who's Who in Professional Speaking: The Meeting Planner's Guide*
○ a listing in the association's web site directory
○ subscriptions to the NSA's audio and print magazines
○ access to purchase of specially packaged audio and visual tapes on speaking techniques
○ certification (after you've qualified) as a Certified Professional Speaker, which is impressive on advertising and promotional materials, but is also not that easy to get—you must earn it

Traits of the Trade

Hey, kids! Take this fun quiz and find out if you've got what it takes to become a seminar professional.

1. *My idea of a fun evening is:*
   a. watching infomercials on late-night TV to see how the pitchmen perform public speaking
   b. snuggling up with a hot toddy and a rough draft of my advertising copy
   c. cruising around town singing "You Talk Too Much"

2. *Here's how I usually send Christmas gifts to relatives who live out-of-state:*
   a. wait until December 24th, stuff the gifts into old grocery bags with the addresses scribbled in crayon, then rush down to the post office and stand in a huge, snaky line with all the other procrastinators and hope my gifts arrive on time and intact
   b. wrap my gifts carefully in specially selected packaging no later than December 10th, call my predesignated FedEx or UPS courier (I've already checked to see which is cheaper and faster), and then follow up to make sure the gifts have arrived on time and intact
   c. hope no one notices I forgot to send gifts

3. *Here's how I manage my library books:*
   a. return them as soon as I receive the first overdue notice
   b. carefully note the due date and return them on or before that date
   c. try to get them out from under the sofa when I receive the collection letter from the city attorney's office

4. *When I am asked to speak in front of a group, I:*
   a. politely decline on the grounds that I have a chronic, contagious disease
   b. accept with delight and immediately get to work preparing my talk
   c. suddenly realize I have an important—and much-appreciated—appointment with my IRS auditor

5. *I would describe my self-motivational abilities as follows:*
   a. I manage to get things done sooner or later.
   b. I love setting and meeting goals and accomplishing tasks!
   c. My self-starter frequently sticks.

Answers: If you chose b for each answer, then you passed with flying colors! You've got what it takes to become a seminar production pro. You're organized, an efficient time manager, and self-motivated.

(featuring candy gummy fish), and other delightful ways to get employers' messages across.

Future Forecast

The seminar professionals interviewed for this book have put their own highly individual and creative stamps on their seminar businesses. You can—and should—do the same. But in addition to personal background, creativity, start-up costs and annual revenues, there's one more thing to consider: the industry prognosis. Will there be a need for seminar production well into the 21st century?

The outlook is optimistic. The number of meetings is increasing, says professional speaker Daniel Burrus, a noted technology forecaster and business strategist and member of the National Speakers Association. Burrus explains that the reason lies in the astounding amount of data being created in our world and the fact that all that data has to be translated into human terms. "Information is static," he says. "Communicating is dynamic." And one of the best ways of communicating is through seminars. Mark Sanborn, president of the National Speakers Association, puts it another way. "A seminar leader," he says, "is an information broker."

The only issues that could negatively impact the industry—and do so very dramatically, Burrus contends—are another major terrorist attack or a global biological epidemic like SARS. Either of these scenarios would have a significant effect on travel, on which the seminar industry depends.

The meetings industry suffered for the first 18 months after 9/11, Burrus says, but is now swinging back into balance. Sanborn agrees: "The number of meetings is back to pre-9/11 levels," he says. And, as he advised at the start of this chapter, "There's a future in the industry for any entrepreneur with a timely topic."

It's always possible that travel could become a traumatic issue. If it did, the smart seminar professional could segue into virtual presentations. (See "The Armchair Seminar" on page 64 in Chapter 4.) It's possible that big business could make a major about-face and start upsizing (as opposed to the current practice of downsizing), which could eliminate a lot of outsourced training programs. But since the smart seminar professional will probably always find a niche to fill, the future of the industry is bright.

So fasten your seatbelt, bring your tray table to the upright position, and let's start on your learning curve. Next chapter: market research!

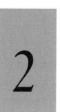

2

On with the Show

Market Research

Every business needs consumers for its products or services to, as the Vulcans so eloquently put it, live long and prosper. Now that you know what running a seminar business entails, you need to plan or target your market, determining who your potential clients will be, what areas you'll draw from, and what specific topics and programs you'll offer to attract them.

This is an important phase in the master seminar profession building project. The proper market research can help boost your business into a true profit center, and the more research you do and the better prepared you are before you officially send out your first materials or place that first ad, the less floundering you're likely to do.

This chapter, therefore, homes in on market research tips and techniques for the budding seminar entrepreneur. First up:

Defining Your Market

To be successful in the seminar business, you'll need to target your market—decide what topics you'll specialize in and who your audience will be. A knock-'em-dead program on "Real-Life X-Files" isn't likely to sell to the Lawrence Welk crowd, and a super seminar on "Osteoarthritis And You" will leave Gen Xers cold. So you'll need to match your subject and your audience.

Every topic on the market can be targeted to a specific group, but some will have a broader appeal than others. Seminars on self-improvement, for instance, generally interest people from all social and economic levels and types of employment, while programs on football fever and ribbon embroidery have a much narrower audience appeal.

Something Fishy

The best way to start is by thinking about what you know, what you enjoy and what your potential customers need or want. Then test your ideas against the following:

- *Your topics must be things you or your presenters are knowledgeable and enthusiastic about.* It's difficult to sell other people on a subject that bores you silly, so your first task is to decide what topic or topics interest and excite you. Make sure it's something that you—or your speakers, if you plan to use others—are knowledgeable about and experienced in. This will give you both confidence and credibility.

  If you're a gung-ho snorkeler or scuba diver and you want to excite and enthuse other people about our planet's vast underwater wilderness, go for it! You could give:

  - motivational talks based on the joy and wonder you've experienced on your dives

Bright Idea

Give your topics high-concept titles. High-concept is a Hollywood term meaning a script idea that gets its point across in a few short words, but it works in the seminar biz, too. Try for kicky, interest-provoking titles like "Working Cool for Employees in the Hot Seat," which is much more intriguing than "Teaching Employees To React Better Under Stress." Right?

- motivational talks based on the courage and camaraderie you've experienced as a Navy SEAL
- environmental seminars based on marine ecology
- workshops on snorkeling or diving
- travel talks on the best snorkeling or diving adventure cruises

But if the thought of saltwater makes you seasick and fish turn you green around the gills, then don't make waves. Your neighbor or spouse may think it's a swell idea, but you probably won't succeed. Instead, find something you understand and enjoy.

Smart Tip Tip...

The American Society for Training and Development offers lots of information and assistance for the seminar professional. (After all, lots of seminars take the form of training sessions.) Check out this organization—you'll find contact information, including a web site chock-full of tidbits, in this book's Appendix.

- *You must have a large customer base from which to draw.* If you know everything there is to know about flies, you find them fascinating and you have a huge collection under glass, that's swell. But you're not going to find many people who will line up to learn about flies. If, on the other hand, you're into fly fishing, you'll have a huge number of enthusiasts all over the world angling for your programs.

- *You must have a well-defined topic.* While you can give a variety of seminars on a variety of subjects, each one must be sharply defined. A sales-oriented seminar on "Ten Ways to Telemarketing Success" will draw a larger crowd than a sales-oriented seminar on "Ten Ways to Telemarketing Success and How to Dress for Successful Closings." Why? Because the former has a focus—it promises potential participants that they'll learn that magic formula for success in one specific area: telemarketing. The latter, on the other hand, is all over the figurative map. It doesn't give a prospective attendee anything to grasp. So make sure you've narrowed your topic to something specific.

- *Your topic must address your audience's wants and needs.* You may have a brilliantly defined topic, a huge customer base, and decades of experience, but if your audience doesn't perceive a need to know, you won't have a winning seminar. You may, for instance, come up with a hard-hitting program on washing dinner dishes—something just about everybody can relate to—and you may have years of on-the-job experience (who doesn't?), but your seminar's going to be a tough sell. Nobody will find this interesting enough or necessary enough to attend.

On the other hand, if you gear your presentation toward household organization or time management, two topics that are really hot, include a section on how to get those dishes done in half the time, and gear it toward the right audience—overstressed

By Invitation Only?

Seminars are characterized as private or public. This doesn't mean that one is hidden behind heavy gates, safe from camera-wielding paparazzi, while the other is staged on a soap box in the public park. The terms refer to who's hosting the program.

A private seminar is one that's sponsored by a corporation or organization and is open only to members of that group, for instance a "Cool Customer Service" workshop presented for employees of the Second National Bank and paid for by the bank, or an "Eating Slim" seminar presented for and paid for by members of the local women's club.

A public seminar is given by the seminar professional and is open to anybody who wants to pay the ticket price, like a program on "Financial Planning for the New Millennium" or a "Be a Better Secretary" workshop presented to secretaries at lots of different firms and paid for by their individual companies.

---

women trying to do it all—you'll probably have a winner. Why? Because your audience will perceive your program as filling a need—teaching them how to keep the home fires burning in half the time.

Winning programs also fill wants. They teach, for instance, how to be richer, happier, more attractive, more motivated or more successful. Even if people don't need these attributes, they want them—badly enough to pay money to learn how to achieve them.

Learning the Ropes

Gail Hahn of Fun*cilitators chose her niche as a natural outgrowth of her "former life" as a recreation professional. A skiing accident led to five surgeries in three years on her knees and feet and an entire year where she could barely walk. But after a dozen years gadding about the world, Hahn found she liked being at home. "I liked having my life back," she says, "knowing that if friends came to visit I didn't have to say, 'I can't be with you because I've used up my annual vacation leave.'"

Tip...

Smart Tip

Meeting planners can be good sources of information on what's hot and what's not. Get acquainted with—or even join—organizations of meeting and special event planners. You'll find contact information for these groups in this book's Appendix.

So the Reston, Virginia, resident decided to start her own homebased business. "What's my unique selling point?" she asked herself. "What can I bottle?" She based the answer—teaching fun and high-energy techniques to businesspeople—on her own personality and the fact that people are always asking her, "Where do you get all your energy?"

Hahn also based her niche topics on the conferences she coordinated for the military while in Germany. "They needed speakers," she explains. "Then the word got out and other people in the military community started asking me to instruct sessions. I also had a ropes course built in Heidelberg and facilitated team-building for groups 50 feet above the ground. I was often asked if I could do similar things without rock-climbing harnesses and inside a hotel ballroom. So I adapted the activities and find that they are very popular in my sessions whether in a conference room, on the beach or at a retreat setting."

Certifiable

One way to trumpet your expertise in your chosen field is with one (or more) certifications. Larry Smith of National Electrical Seminars in Omaha, Nebraska, for instance, is a certified electrical code trainer in 14 states. He has also achieved a CSP (Certified Speaking Professional) designation from the National Speakers Association, which is not easy to obtain.

"It takes five years of consistent quality programming, earning an average of $50,000 per year, serving at least 100 clients and doing an average of 50 programs per year," explains Gail Hahn of Fun*cilitators, who also boasts a CSP designation. "You also have to rate at least an 8 out of 10 on an evaluation the association sends to your past clients to make sure you are providing quality and not just quantity."

"I have a loose-leaf binder full of CSP materials sent back and forth to the National Speakers Association that's 5 inches thick," Smith adds.

Along with her CSP, Hahn also claims certification as a Strength Deployment Inventory Facilitator and a string of other letters after her name: MA, CPRP and CLL (for Master of Arts degree, Certified Parks and Recreation Professional, and Certified Laugh Leader).

"I think these certifications bring a depth to my programs and also a longer pedigree!" says the Reston, Virginia, speaker. "With some of my topics of fun and lightheartedness, I needed to show there is some depth and serious work behind the laughter. I think it's a critical link into why my clients hire me, because of my research, continuing education, and expertise in the field."

Everybody Knows Something

Dr. Jerry Old found that, like Gail's niche, his niche—Vintage People—just sort of developed itself. "For me," he says, "this business 'evolved' without doing much formal research. I was simply doing what I enjoyed and what people wanted. The best market research is what your audiences tell you they want to hear and learn about. I learn as much at every seminar as the clients do. Everyone knows something that can benefit others—you just have to examine your talents and determine what it is."

Mandated Education

Yet another seminar professional who found his niche the natural way is Larry Smith of Omaha, Nebraska-based National Electrical Seminars. "I did just enough market research," he says, "to know that Nebraska, Wyoming, and South Dakota had mandated continuing education for electricians as a requisite for relicensing. Since then, several other states have followed suit. It's a niche market. The most helpful thing was understanding the electrical industry."

The Core Concept

"To be successful at seminars," Nance Cheifetz of Sense of Delight in Novato, California, counsels, "you must know how to market or hook up with someone who does. Understand who your market is; then narrow it down to a niche. You can diversify within that niche." Cheifetz's niche is teaching participants to tap into their sense of delight. She has done keynotes for singles groups and self-esteem programs for children. In the past few years, she's taken her core concept and modified it to fit her corporate clients. "The passion behind the business," she says, "is to bring out the best in people, fun and recognition, and an appreciation of the skill sets that everybody brings to the table."

Dr. Old echoes the idea of tailoring your market to your own particular niche. "I modify my program depending on what the audience wants," explains the Shawnee, Kansas, doctor. "I frequently get asked to speak to groups after dinner or the more standard one-hour speech. Besides 'Vintage People,' I also speak on 'Humor Is Good Medicine and 'Prescription For Success.'" Dr. Old also does a talk adapted to RSVP (Retired and Senior Volunteer Program) members straightforwardly called "Volunteering Is Good Medicine." His seminars on seniors are

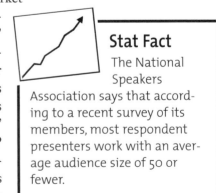

Stat Fact
The National Speakers Association says that according to a recent survey of its members, most respondent presenters work with an average audience size of 50 or fewer.

composed mostly of older adults. "There is, however, an increasing attendance by younger people who are interested in older adults," he says, "which I think is a good trend.

"I'm trying to speak to more sales groups but find this area is harder to break into. Recently I find most companies downsizing, and they are eliminating or reducing their budgets for seminars, at least in this area. Pharmaceutical companies are the exception."

Choosing Your Audience

OK, you've chosen a specialty, you've decided on a topic or group of topics, and you're rarin' to go. Good! But your work's not done. Now you need to decide just who your audiences or participants will be. Choose from among this list of candidates:

- corporate businesses
- associations
- professionals
- salespeople
- social groups
- the masses

Corporate Businesses

There are several immediate benefits to the world of corporate seminars. One is that people are more likely to attend a program when the company foots the bill than when they have to pay for it themselves. Another is that people often view a seminar as a good opportunity to play hooky guilt-free—it's a built-in excuse to get out of the office for a while, so they're eager to attend. A third is that the IRS allows people to take a deduction for any expenses incurred while maintaining or improving professional skills—and that includes seminars and workshops. So even though the company usually pays all costs associated with seminars, executives who pay their own expenses can get a tax break while traveling or dining out. Who could lose?

You can target business audiences by company size, specialty, or number of employees. Once you've decided on the type of business, you'll need to define your target market in

> **Smart Tip** *Tip...*
>
> Business seminars are perennially popular, especially now that so much of the corporate world has downsized. When companies can no longer afford to hire inhouse trainers, they turn to outside sources. And one of those can be you!

Any Topic Under the Sun

Business seminars and workshops can encompass just about any topic under the sun. If you have a background as a CEO, you might talk on taking your company global or into the internet age. If you are (or have been) a stellar secretary, you might give workshops on "Organizing Your Executive Officer," phone skills, or overcoming office ennui. Depending on your interests and experience, you can give programs on human resources issues, computer smarts, safety, security, stress, environmental concerns within the office, multicultural communications, or customer service—to name just a few. And in a world where men are from Mars and women are from Venus, everybody's interested in learning about interplanetary, er, intergender communications.

greater detail by determining who within the industry would most benefit from your seminar.

Flower Power

Let's say you've been a florist for years and you know everything there is to know about advertising. Your customers not only buy flowers for all the usual occasions like Valentine's Day and Mother's Day, but for Halloween, Fourth of July, Armed Forces Day, and Bad Hair Day. Other florists are always asking how you achieve these stellar results. So you decide to create and market a "Flower Power: Advertising For Florists" seminar.

You know that the entire floral industry is composed of lots of segments: growers, wholesalers, suppliers, and retailers. You choose to target retailers as your major market because that's the group that can most benefit from your program, but you'll also target wholesalers as a secondary market—once they know your secrets, they can improve their business by using your techniques to sell to retailers.

OK, this is good. But you're not done yet. Next you'll need to decide where your target participants will be located. Do you want to go after every retail florist in the country—requiring a major marketing budget—or will you start with one area of the country, like the Southeast, where you just happen to live?

You choose the Southeast because you won't have to travel as much as if you choose the opposite end of the country, you're comfortable with the mindset, and you know that when you're traveling you'll always be able to find a restaurant that serves grits for breakfast.

Organizational Genius

If we hit the "rewind" button and make you a corporate whiz kid instead of a green thumb type, we can say that you are an organizational genius, the envy of all your co-workers because your desk doesn't look like a tornado just hit and you can find all those three-year-old reports at a moment's notice. So now you decide to market "Audaciously Organized" seminars to train the filing-impaired.

Now comes your next decision: Will you slant your seminar toward power-suited CEOs, middle managers or working woman (or man) secretaries? Each of these groups is going to have a different agenda, different needs, and a different take on life. You can develop three different seminars—one for each group—or you can target one. But you'll need to choose.

Then you'll need to make the same sort of decision as you did in your florist incarnation: Where will your market be located? You'll have to choose a part of the country to target first, and you might also want to choose a business size—will you go with the AT&T-sized mega-corporation, with SOHO (small office/home office) types or with companies somewhere in between?

Associations

The corporate world isn't the only one out there. There are also thousands of national associations in the United States, many of which have local chapters, and all these groups hold hundreds of meetings, conventions or conferences each year. What sorts of associations? Everything from the National Restaurant Association to the Master Brewers Association to the National Association of Margarine Manufacturers and the National Pasta Association. Then there's the National Association of Gifted Children and the American Association of Retired Persons, the North American Nursery and Landscape Association and the American Horse Show Association, the Audubon Society and the Sierra Club. And more. Lots more. In just about every category you can imagine (and some you might not).

Desperately Seeking Speakers

All these groups need professional assistance for their conferences and conventions: keynote speakers to kick things off or wrap them up as well as luncheon and dinner speakers, session trainers, and presenters for a wide variety of workshops and seminars. A single convention can bring in tremendous revenues for an association

Smart Tip

Tip...

Schedule a public seminar at a hotel to coincide with an association's big meeting. Then offer association members discount tickets. This gives members a perk and gives you a greater audience and more ticket sales.

if it can convince its members to attend. So it's in the association administrator's best interests to check the convention in at a swanky destination like Las Vegas, New York or Disney World (depending on the group's definition of "swanky"), but also to book speakers and programs with drawing power. Which means there are all sorts of groups out there desperately seeking you!

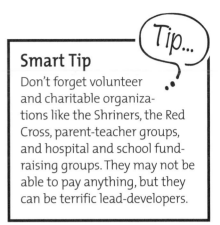

Smart Tip

Don't forget volunteer and charitable organizations like the Shriners, the Red Cross, parent-teacher groups, and hospital and school fund-raising groups. They may not be able to pay anything, but they can be terrific lead-developers.

You'll have to do your market research here, too, to find out what associations are out there and what programs will appeal to them. If you're already a member of an association, you've got a head start. You should have a good idea of what your cohorts will be interested in. If you don't belong (and even if you do), think not only about what these groups may be looking for, but whether the idea you may already have in mind can work in the association's setting. Motivational topics, for instance, can be tailored to various groups, while topics like "Oleomargarines—Fat Or Fun?" will only play in the margarine market, or in another group with similar food and health concerns.

Professionals

Among all those national associations, there are hundreds of professional organizations—everything from the American Bar Association and the American Medical Association to the National Association of Professional Organizers and the National Association of Broadcasters. And again, more—lots more! A bonus for targeting these groups is that many professionals—from nurses and social workers to real estate brokers and accountants, to name just a few—are required to engage in continuing education. If you get your programs counted as partial continuing education units, you generate an inherent need for them, and thus for you.

Stat Fact

According to a recent survey, the National Speakers Association says its polled members each conducted more than 200 speaking engagements in one recent year.

Designing your seminars and workshops to count as continuing education is a smart move, but it's not the only way to go when targeting professionals. As you do when targeting corporations and associations, think about how your ideas, enthusiasm, and experience can be tailored to programs that will appeal to these groups. It doesn't have to be industry-specific education. Professionals of any stripe appreciate seminars on motivation, inspiration, humor, investments, and personal improvement. Figure out what you can do to make yours special.

Salespeople

We've given salespeople a category all their own, even though they're technically corporate types or professionals. Why? Because these folks are traditionally terrific candidates for seminars and workshops. Their efficiency is measured by the number of sales they make and the number of clients they retain, yet theirs is a job where they're frequently told "no" in very certain terms. So they're a ready and willing market for topics like "Chill Out and Make Those Cold Calls Hot" and "How to Make Lifetime Customers."

> ### Smart Tip
>
> **Tip...**
>
> When you think organization, think service organizations, too. How about your local Kiwanis, Jaycees, and Rotary Club? Like volunteer groups, they may not pay much (or anything), but they're a terrific foot in the door, give you "free" experience, and could give you leads to fee gigs.

Social Groups

Don't underestimate the benefits of targeting small, local groups that have nothing to do with sales or business. Churches and temples, senior centers, and men's and women's clubs can make terrific audiences along with singles clubs, single parents' groups, local sports clubs, civic organizations, networking groups, writers' groups, book clubs, and garden clubs. Their budgets are likely to be smaller than those of corporate America or national associations, but you can gain invaluable experience, both in working with an audience and in market research. Have your participants fill out an evaluation page after your program—you'll learn lots about what you did right, what you did not so right, and what to incorporate or delete for your next seminar.

You can also gain prime exposure from these gigs. You never know what contacts you'll make that will lead to more lucrative engagements down the line.

The Masses

> ### Stat Fact
>
> According to the U.S. Bureau of Labor Statistics, more than 13 million people were employed in sales occupations in one recent year, so this is a major seminar market.

Another valuable—and voluminous—market is the mass market, or the public at large, which has a voracious appetite for self-help programs of every description. Take a look at the magazines on display at your local supermarket and at the bestselling books on view in your local bookstore. You'll get a quick idea of what people want: how to make money or save money, how to afford a home, how to find true love or save a marriage, how to raise successful kids, how to be successful themselves, how to deal with stress, how to get healthy, how to lose weight, how to gain self-confidence, and again—the real key to all the rest—how to get and remain motivated.

Researching Your Market

You've decided what types of seminars or workshops you'll specialize in and who your participants will be. Good! But you're still not finished with your market research. Now you'll need to go directly to your potential customers to find out how they really feel about the materials you plan to offer. Would they attend? How much would they pay? Where does your price ceiling lie?

Let's say you're a 20-year veteran of the public school system and you've spent your career teaching French, Spanish, Italian, world history, and geography. You're a travel buff and you've bravely led many a senior-class European tour as well as done the Europe-on-a-budget thing as often as possible on your own. You see early retirement looming on the horizon, and while you don't want to extend your tenure with the county school board, you don't want to lose the income and fulfillment of a career.

So you start planning a new career giving travel-based seminars: one for business travelers, one for vacationing retirees, and one for people who want to learn more about their faith by putting religious history into a geographical perspective. This way you can combine your knowledge of teaching, geography, and romance languages into a series of programs that will be valuable for your participants and yourself.

You think this is a keen idea. But how do you know if anybody else will think so or be interested enough to actually pay for it?

Smart Tip

Tip...

Individuals are not likely to pay as much for your programs as corporations or major associations, but it all adds up. If you can come up with a topic that will get people fired up and eager to attend, you can sell enough tickets to make each seminar well worth your while.

Up Close and Personal

One way is by getting up close and personal—and cozy—with a focus group. This is an informal gathering between you and a medley of potential seminar participants, usually five to 12 people. Try to hold several different focus groups—the more responses you can get, the better. You can invite family (though they may be biased on your behalf), friends, friends of friends, co-workers, and colleagues in clubs or organizations you belong to. Keep in mind, however, that your focus groups should be composed of people who will have some connection with your proposed seminar. For instance, when researching the business traveler program, you would want to invite people who are known intercontinental business travelers—your co-workers or those of your spouse or sibling, or people from a local business organization. Acquaintances whose only business travel is taking the cross-town bus can be left out.

Once you've gotten your focus group assembled and you've distributed some sort of refreshment (always a nice touch), you have a captive audience to respond to your most pressing market concerns. Hand out questionnaires, have plenty of pens and pencils on tap, and encourage discussion. You'll learn more than you can imagine!

> **Bright Idea**
>
> Be sure to collect the names and addresses of all focus group participants. They'll be the seeds of your in-house mailing list, which you'll use for advertising and marketing (and which you'll learn all about in Chapters 10 and 11).

Delve into the sample focus group questionnaire starting on page 33 for an idea of how to formulate your own question-and-answer sessions. Obviously, your questions will relate to your own target market. Instead of travel and geography, you might be asking about gardening or interpersonal communications. Ask as many questions as you feel your group can comfortably handle (don't try holding people captive until three in the morning). But keep your questions focused (this is, after all, a focus group) on your objective: finding out what potential audiences will want to learn, what they'll pay and what seminar titles will draw them in.

Calling All Attendees

Telephone surveys are another market research tool, although not quite as up close and personal. Some folks are delighted to answer questions—after all, it's always flattering to have somebody seek your opinion. Others in this era of caller ID are wary of unsolicited calls and reluctant to squander valuable time on telephone strangers. Unless you've got thick skin, it can be a little difficult to make cold calls to people you don't know and pick their brains. But if you can home in on people in a specific audience, say retiree vacationers, and explain why you're calling, you'll have a much better shot at getting relaxed responses.

You can use your focus group questionnaire as the basis of your telephone survey, but keep it short and to the point.

Where do you get the phone numbers? If you belong to an association or organization and it just happens to be affiliated with your target market, you've got it made. You may already have a directory packed with names and phone numbers at hand. If not, you may be able to beg, borrow, or buy a directory from the organization's main office. If your specialty is something more general, like motivation and self-esteem, you might still start off with the members of your club or group. Your common membership will act as the proverbial foot in the door.

If you don't know anybody and you don't belong to any groups, how about a church roster or neighborhood association? Use your imagination!

Direct-Mail Dazzle

Direct mail is a terrific market research tool. You can use the same lists or directories you'd use in your telephone surveys (but don't attack the same people with both phone and mail questionnaires—choose one form or the other).

What do you say in your mail survey? You can ask the same types of questions you've got in your focus group questionnaire. But keep in mind that people are unlikely to return a mail survey unless you offer them an incentive. So get creative! Extend an invitation to be put on your mailing list. Give them a coupon for 10 percent off their first seminar, or 10 percent off any of the goodies from your back-of-the-room sales.

Free or Fee

The best things in life aren't always free—or at least not in audiences' perceptions. Sometimes people equate a free seminar as not worth their time and attention. A program aimed at wealthy investors, for instance, might do better to charge a nominal fee, while one targeted at budget-conscious retirees might do just fine as a freebie. You'll have to figure out on your own whether this applies to your potential customers based on your knowledge of them and of your topics.

Whoever your attendees are, be sure to offer a questionnaire after your seminar. Take a look at the sample starting on page 33 for an idea of what to ask and how to ask it. Be sure to take notes on everything about your audience, including:

- age
- dress
- interaction (or lack thereof) with speakers
- points that catch their interest (or fail to)
- whether they arrive alone, in pairs or in groups

All of this information will help you paint a true portrait of your ideal audience and what you can do to attract them.

Just the Facts, Ma'am!

Besides going directly to your potential participants for market research, you'll also want, as Jack Webb on "Dragnet" would say, "just the

> **Bright Idea**
> If telephone cold-calling leaves you chilled to the bone, try hiring a college student. This age group is old enough to sound mature but young enough to bring enthusiasm to the job. Just make sure your ace assistant knows what questions to ask and why you're asking, and can take good (and legible) notes.

Free and Easy

The free seminar is a favorite market research tool among the seminar profession set. This is where you really put your ideas to the test. Design and prepare your program, and then invite an audience—you can use the sampling groups we've discussed, people who already have some sort of interest in your subject matter. You can also advertise in your local newspaper and in freebie publications that may be at your disposal, like church, company or association newsletters.

Then comes the heart-fluttering moment when you discover how many people actually show up to hear your seminar. Gauging attendance is one way to determine what sort of crowd you can draw. But just as important—or perhaps even more so—you can have your audience fill out after-seminar evaluations (like the one starting on page 35) and grade your work. Scary, but invaluable!

facts, ma'am," all that good old statistical information, as you did in your florist incarnation. How many retail florists are there, for instance, in the United States, in the Southeast or in greater metropolitan Atlanta? How many retirees with a sufficient income to travel are there in the Midwest? How many real estate professionals are there in Anchorage, Alaska? The answers will give you an idea of just how many potential participants there are for your programs and if that number is large enough to be lucrative.

You can get all this sort of information, and much more, from a variety of sources, including:

- *The public library*. Reference librarians can be fantastically helpful with this sort of thing. All you have to do is call and tell the librarian that you need to know how many medical professionals, fly fishermen or disabled children under age 14 there are in the United States. She'll look up the information and call you back with the answer. Or you can go into the library and dig through whole books of demographic statistics yourself, unearthing more facts and figures than you could use in a quadruple round of Trivial Pursuit.

- *The internet*. A world library at your fingertips! If you're not yet net-savvy, make becoming so a priority—you'll have

Bright Idea

Don't forget to have participants fill out a guest book. You'll want all the names and addresses you can collect for future mailings.

access to all sorts of demographics without ever leaving your desk. For starters, check in with the U.S. Census Bureau at www.census.gov (yes, they collect all that data for a reason—here's your chance to take advantage of it) and the Department of Commerce at www.doc.gov.

- *Organizations and associations.* What better places to go for information on your specific market? If you are targeting senior citizens, for example, you could contact the American Association of Retired Persons for a count of its members; for a count of primary school teachers, you would talk to the folks at state and regional teachers associations.

Shopping the Competition

No matter how well you target your market and plan your seminars, you're going to face competition of some sort from some avenue. This is OK—a little competition is healthy. If you do your homework properly and structure your programs intelligently, your company will shine despite—or because of—your rivals' lights.

The time to scrutinize those rivals is during your market research phase. What are they doing that's absolutely perfect? What can you successfully emulate? What are they doing that you can do better? What can you offer that will draw customers away from them and to you? How can you answer all these questions? By performing these research tasks:

- *Go ahead and shop—the competition, that is.* Attend all the seminars and workshops you can. Study them. What works? What doesn't? And why?

- *Read every book written by well-known (and not-so-well-known) speaker/authors and analyze them.* Listen to their audiotapes and watch their videos.

- *Check out speakers bureau web sites like the National Speakers Association at www.nsaspeaker.org.* This is a terrific way to check out who's doing what sort of seminars and what topics are popular.

- *Surf your competitors' web sites, which you can often log on to via the speakers bureaus.* Again, study what your rivals are doing. Explore what works and what doesn't— and why.

Focus Group Questionnaire for Business Traveler Seminars

Here's a sample questionnaire to get you thinking about the kinds of things you'll want to ask your focus group participants.

1. How many times a year do you travel out of the country on business?

   _____

2. Which cities and countries do you visit? _____

   _____

3. Do you speak the languages and, if so, are you fluent? In which ones?

   _____

4. What sorts of multicultural difficulties have you encountered? _____

   _____

5. Where do you usually stay? _____

   _____

6. Does your spouse or family ever accompany you? _____

   _____

7. What would you be most interested in learning that would help you on your trips? _____

   _____

8. If you could extend a business trip to include vacation travel, would you be interested? _____

   _____

9. Where would you like to visit? _____

   _____

Focus Group Questionnaire
for Business Traveler Seminars, continued

10. Are you interested in the history of the countries you visit? _____

_____

11. Are you interested in the art or music of the countries you visit? _____

_____

12. Would you be interested in a seminar that would teach you, in a lighthearted and entertaining way, how to think like a native of the countries you visit?

_____

13. How much would you expect to pay for this type of seminar? _____

_____

14. Have you attended a seminar of this type in the past? _____

_____

15. If so, did you find it helpful? Why or why not? _____

_____

_____

16. Please comment on the seminar title "Going Native: How to Succeed in Business by Thinking Like Your French [or Italian or other European] Customer" (love, like, dislike, or hate, and why): _____

_____

_____

17. Please comment on the seminar title "Dinner at Nine: Italian Thinking for the Business Traveler" (love, like, dislike, or hate, and why): _____

_____

_____

Post-Program Evaluation

Thanks for attending our program! Your thoughts and comments are very important to us and will help us make our programs the best they can be. So go ahead—grade us!

1. Did the program give you tools and techniques you can use?
   A   B   C   D   F

2. Was the information presented in an entertaining fashion?
   A   B   C   D   F

3. Was the material new, informative, and thought-provoking?
   A   B   C   D   F

4. What did you like best about the program? _____

   _____

   _____

5. What did you like least? _____

   _____

   _____

6. How did you feel about the length of the program?
   too short   too long   perfect

7. How well did the presenter promote audience participation?
   A   B   C   D   F

8. How would you rate our workbook?
   A   B   C   D   F

9. How would you rate our visual materials (slides, videos, etc.)?
   A   B   C   D   F

10. How would you rate the food and beverage service?
    A   B   C   D   F

Post-Program Evaluation, continued

11. Would you prefer a program with meals included, or do you like to eat on your own? _____

_____

12. Please tell us how you felt about the meeting facilities: _____

_____

_____

13. Would you be interested in attending another of our programs? What topics would appeal to you? _____

_____

_____

14. We like feedback! Please give us any other comments you feel would be helpful: _____

_____

_____

15. May we use your comments in our advertising or marketing materials?

_____

If yes, thank you! May we have your name and company name and address?

_____

_____

16. Would you like to receive mailings on our future programs? Terrific! Please provide your name and mailing address: _____

_____

_____

	3

Designing Your Theater
Choosing a Name and a Structure

K, you've done your market research. You've decided on your topics and your participants. Terrific! Now you'll need to design a tight, sturdy "theater" for your new company, a structure that will keep it not only lookin' good, but solid enough to weather anything life might dish out. In this chapter we guide you through that process from

choosing a company name and a legal structure to hiring professional help and beyond.

Name that Business

Every business, like every child, has to have a name—and you should devote as much thought to choosing an appellation for your company as you would for your human offspring. After all, you plan to have your business baby around for a long time. You want a name you can be proud of, one that identifies it—and by extension, you— as worthy of your customers' confidence. You also want a name that gives your customers and clients—both individual participants and sponsors like associations and corporations—a clear portrait of who you are and what topics you're selling. Use the brainstorming worksheet on page 42 to generate ideas for your business name.

Larry Smith chose his company name based on several criteria. "I wanted the company to be operative nationally," says the Omaha, Nebraska, entrepreneur. "This dictated the first word, 'National.' Electrical seminars is what we do. National Electrical Seminars conducts seminars

> ## Smart Tip
> Always get a name, department and phone extension when you call someone in officialdom. This can save you hours of re-explanation if you need to call again. Plus, you might make a friend who can help with other matters later on down the line.

At First Glance

Since your customers' first contact with your company will probably be on paper, you'll need to provide them with a bold company image. This means that your visual image—the colors, graphics, typefaces, and paper stocks you choose for everything from stationery to brochures to mailing labels—is important to how they perceive you. If your seminars focus on kids, for instance, go all-out for a logo that says children with bright primary colors and a bouncy, exuberant type style. If you're talking travel, splash your materials with "travel stickers" or tower images—Eiffel, Pisa, London. You can design just about everything with your trusty desktop-publishing program. But keep in mind that you're selling not only your special expertise, energy level, and ambience, but an image of soundness. You want potential clients to know they're in good hands when they hire you.

Smart Tip

Tip...

If your first-choice domain name's been taken, get creative. But not so creative that your domain name has no relation to your company name. If your company is called Motivations Plus, for instance, and there is already a www.motivations.com, try something like www.mplus.com or www.motivate.com.

based on the National Electrical Code name recognition. I will also, sometime in the future, sell the company. It will be much more marketable as National Electrical Seminars than it would be with some other cute name."

Gail Hahn in Reston, Virginia, chose a name that reflects the theme of her seminars—building energy by having fun. Thus, "Fun*cilitators," complete with a kicky asterisk in the middle.

"My company name is a no-brainer," Dr. Jerry Old of Shawnee, Kansas, says. "I used my name."

For some top-notch ideas on choosing your own moniker, check out the seminar companies in our Appendix. You'll want to make yours as individual as you are, but these will get those creative gears turning.

Eminent Domain

If you plan to have a web site, you'll need to register your domain name, that www.whatever thing people type in to access your virtual office. There can be only one domain name per company, so you'll have to think up several versions of the name you want in case one's already been taken.

You can register your domain name yourself on a registration/web hosting site like Network Solutions (www.networksolutions.com) or Register.com (www.register.com); or you can have your web site designer do it for you. Do-it-yourself registration prices range from $15 to $70 for two years.

On Your Own

To appease those picky IRS people, your business must have a structure. You can operate it as a sole proprietorship, a partnership or a corporation, with variations thereon. Many seminar professional newbies go with the simplest version, the sole proprietorship. If you'll be starting out on your own, you may choose the same option—it's the least complicated and the least expensive. You can always switch to another format later on, if and when you take on partners and/or employees.

Laying Your Foundation

There's more to laying the foundation of your business than choosing a name. You'll need to decide on a legal structure, check into zoning regulations and insurance coverage, and line up an attorney and an accountant—all the nitty-gritty stuff that will give your company a solid base on which to build.

Home Zoned Home

If you plan to work from home, you'll want to check into zoning regulations. Since your business will be virtual—conducted by mail, phone, and web site—you won't need signs pinpointing your location. And since it's unlikely you'll have customers knocking at your door, you won't need to worry about parking restrictions. But it's still a smart idea to play it safe. Find out from your city government whether any permits are necessary, and if they are, file them. If you need a zoning variance, apply for it.

While you are interfacing with your local authorities, ask about a business license. This generally consists of filling out a simple form and paying a nominal annual fee. Again, it's easier to get the license upfront than to ignore it and have it worrying at the back of your brain.

Attorneys and Plumbers

Attorneys are like plumbers—you do not want to think about them until you need one. But as a business owner, you should have a good attorney on call, someone who knows small business. You will want your attorney to check over any contracts you write with manufacturers, suppliers, publishers or video producers for back-of-the-room sales materials, and to advise you on the fine points of literary or entertainment law. You won't need to call your attorney every week, or even every month. But there is no point in waiting until you have a problem to establish a relationship.

Along with that on-call attorney, you'll want to look into hiring an accountant to fill out those tax returns and advise you of any special ways you can save money with your business structure.

And don't forget your insurance agent! He can be an invaluable source of information and expertise. If you'll be homebased, you'll need to find out if your homeowners' package covers your business assets, inventory, and equipment, or if you need additional coverage. If you're based outside the home, you need coverage for these same

Stat Fact
According to a recent National Speakers Association survey, a whopping 82.2 percent of its respondents work out of a home office.

Right On!

If you plan to sell self-published back-of-the-room books, pamphlets or other materials, you'll want to copyright them. You can copyright cartoon characters, sculptures, paintings, plays, maps, songs, scripts, photographs, and poems.

You can copyright your material all on your own simply by adding a copyright notice on the material. Three elements make up the copyright notice:

1. the word "copyright," the copyright symbol (©) or the abbreviation "copr."
2. the name of the owner of the copyright (that's you)
3. the year of first publication

Here's what a copyright should look like: © by John Doe, 2004

For copyrights of sound recordings like CDs and audio cassettes, change the © to a ℗. The "P" is for "phonorecord."

If you want to get really formal, you can file a copyright with the U.S. government. For information, contact the Library of Congress, Copyright Office at Publications Section, LM-455, 101 Independence Ave. SE, Washington, DC 20559-6000, call (202) 707-3000, or find them at www.copyright.gov.

items, as well as your physical location. If you plan to hire employees, you may need workers' compensation insurance.

Business Name Brainstorming Worksheet

List three ideas based on the seminars or workshops you plan to provide (i.e., internet marketing, interpersonal communications, community gardening).

1. _____

2. _____

3. _____

List three ideas combining a favorite theme with your planned topics (i.e., marketing for the global village, Tarzan/Jane thinking, food for the community/food for thought).

1. _____

_____

2. _____

_____

3. _____

_____

After you've decided which name you like best, have you:

❑ tried it aloud to make sure it's easily understood and pronounced? (Has it passed muster with your family? Have you had a friend call to see how it sounds over the phone?)

❑ checked your local Yellow Pages to make sure the same or similar name is not already listed?

❑ checked with your local business name authority to make sure it's available?

4

Box Office Management
Figuring Your Finances

That old refrain "The best things in life are free" does not quite apply when you're starting a business. This chapter dips into the murky waters of budgeting, financing, and operating costs and, like chlorine, clears them up.

Start-Up Costs

One of the many nifty things about the seminar business is that its start-up costs are comparatively low. You've got the advantage of homebased ability, which cuts office lease expenses down to nothing. Except for any back-of-the-room (BOR) products you may choose to develop, you've got no inventory. And even if you've got inventory, you won't need fancy display cabinets or kicky décor. Your major financial outlay will go toward office equipment, marketing and promotion, and—if you're doing public seminars—your site facilities. And if you're like many moderns, you've already got the most expensive piece of office equipment: a computer system.

But let's take it from the top. The following is a breakdown of everything—from heavy investment pieces to flyweight items—you'll want to get up and running:

- computer system with modem and printer
- fax machine
- internet/e-mail service
- web site design and marketing
- software
- electronic credit card processing
- bulk mail permit
- market research
- phone
- voice mail, answering machine, or answering service
- stationery and office supplies
- shipping and packaging supplies

Splashy Start

A grand opening is a terrific way to kick off your new venture with a splash and let everyone know you're open for business. Invite friends, family, vendors, and suppliers, people from your mailing list who live in the area, and local news media. If you'll be homebased, get creative with the site for your bash. If your new baby is a golfing seminar, for instance, hold your party at a local golf course.

Be sure to have each well-wisher sign a guest book and leave his or her address—free information! Give out brochures or other sales pieces and perhaps a small freebie from your product line.

- postage
- initial inventory

You can add all kinds of goodies of varying degrees of necessity to this list, and we'll cover them all in Chapter 7, which features a sort of shopping bonanza. For example, a copier is a plus. It's also nice to have bona fide office furniture: a swiveling, rolling, tweedy upholstered chair with lumbar support; gleaming file cabinets that really lock; and real oak bookshelves.

But let's consider that you're starting from absolute scratch. You can always set up your computer on your kitchen table or on a card table in a corner of the bedroom. You can stash files in cardboard boxes. It's not glamorous, but it'll suffice until you get your business steaming ahead.

Computer Basics

For a basic computer system—hard drive, monitor, mouse, modem, and printer— you should allocate in the range of $1,000 to $1,500, depending on how high-tech you go. We'll go over the various permutations in Chapter 7, but this will give you a figure to pencil in for starters.

Go Anywhere

A good internet and e-mail service is a must for the seminar professional. With the power of the World Wide Web at your command, you can go anywhere on the globe instantaneously—you can research your competition, communicate with customers, and garner market information from worldwide sources, all from the comfort of your own desktop. And it's cheap! Most ISPs range from $20 to $25 per month, depending on the provider and type of service, and give you unlimited access to the web and to e-mail.

Internet Source

Four of the five seminar professionals we talked with for this book have their own web sites. Like many elements of the seminar business, the costs for putting up and maintaining a company web site can vary considerably. If you plan to go the web site route and you're lucky enough to have a computer brain in the family, or if you take the time to become your own computer expert, you can pencil in a zero under web design and construction costs.

Web design and hosting fees may be higher in larger urban areas. Shop around. It doesn't

Bright Idea
Put a guest book on your site and ask signers if they'd like to receive a free newsletter or tip sheet. It creates interest and goodwill, and builds your mailing list.

matter if you're in Atlanta, Chicago, or L.A. You can hire a webmaster in Pipsqueak, South Dakota, and work with him as easily as if he were next door.

What can you expect to pay if you outsource your web site construction? You can pencil in from $10 to $85 per month—plus setup fees—for a package that includes web hosting and site building as well as other features like e-mail. Or, if you've got the talent, the temperament, and the aptitude, you can set up your site yourself and pay only web hosting, with prices beginning at $25 to $50 per month.

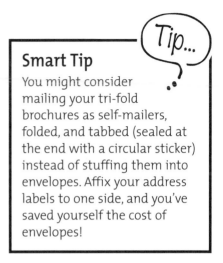

Smart Tip

You might consider mailing your tri-fold brochures as self-mailers, folded, and tabbed (sealed at the end with a circular sticker) instead of stuffing them into envelopes. Affix your address labels to one side, and you've saved yourself the cost of envelopes!

To go the do-it-yourself route, you'll need to learn HTML (that's hypertext markup language), which usually takes a fair amount of teeth-gnashing to master, but once you've got it, you can make all the changes you like whenever you like without having to rely on an outside source. As a third option, you may be lucky enough to have a friend or relative who'll put up your site in exchange for lawn-mowing, baby-sitting, or a steady supply of homebaked cookies.

The Software Skinny

Although your computer will fill that silent partner/co-pilot slot with panache, it needs software to give it all those brains. You'll need a good, strong word-processing program, a desktop-publishing program, a database program for tracking clients and

---

Start Me Up, Part 1

Start-up costs vary with the type of seminar business and the entrepreneurs who design them. "My start-up expenses included a computer, fax, and software," Dr. Jerry Old says of his part-time seminar business in Shawnee, Kansas. "I used a home office, which was converted from a den. Total start-up, including fliers, postage, and advertising, was around $5,000."

Larry Smith, the electrical code trainer in Omaha, Nebraska, is a full-timer. "I started with $10,000," he says. "The goal from the start was to make the company pay for itself, not to borrow or to tap into savings."

Start Me Up, Part 2

Gail Hahn decided that her startup goal was to get her Reston, Virginia, company up and running quickly. "To get up to speed very fast," she explains, "I produced three videos and four audiotapes, manufactured some other customized products, published a book and many articles, and created a web site in the first year and a half. So it cost me more than it would someone who started out just speaking.

"Since I was single," she adds, "I needed to ensure I would be able to make a living at it because I didn't have the safety net of a working spouse. I guess it cost around $18,000 in start-up expenses. I had taken an entrepreneurs class from the Small Business Development Center and had a complete business plan in which I calculated it would cost me about $9,000. I thought I had padded the budget, but it was—as they warned—about double what I thought it would cost me.

"I'm laughing all the way to the bank now," Hahn says, "since my classmates and the two instructors said my one-person business with about five profit centers would never fly and that I couldn't possibly handle it. They underestimated my commitment, my goals, and the precedents that many of my female colleagues have set doing exactly the same thing."

attendees, and an accounting program. Again, this is a subject we'll discuss in depth in Chapter 7. For start-up purposes, let's say that you'll want to allocate from $300 to $1,000.

When you purchase your new computer, you can often buy it preloaded with word-processing and accounting programs that will suit your needs. If you negotiate wisely, you might save valuable software dollars.

Charge It!

You don't have to start with electronic credit card processing, but it helps, especially if you plan on doing public seminars. You can take credit card payments for advance ticket sales—and back-of-the-room products—on your web site, over the phone or from faxed information. And with a portable electronic card terminal, a PDA (personal digital assistant like a Palm Pilot), or even some mobile phones, you can take charge card payments at the event.

Most traditional banks, like the ones at the strip mall or downtown where most people deposit their weekly payroll checks, balk at setting up merchant accounts for SOHO (small office/home office) and seminar businesses because they fear a heavy credit risk. But more and more merchant card service firms are springing up that cater specifically to SOHO and internet entrepreneurs. Shop around—especially on the web—and you'll find a variety to choose from.

What can you expect to pay for an electronic card terminal? Fees depend on several factors:

- the company you go with
- the type of business you're building
- your personal credit history

> ⚠ **Beware!**
> If the merchant card service doesn't state upfront on its web site or other literature that it represents a legitimate bank, it probably isn't legitimate, either.

Some merchant banks consider seminar promotion a "safe" enterprise, unlike, for instance, selling those dime-a-minute phone cards or deeds to the Brooklyn Bridge (businesses that will probably get a lot of charge-backs, or returns). So you'll pay a relatively low discount rate, which is the rate you pay per transaction. Others take into account the type of seminars you'll offer. Make-a-million-dollars real estate and financial programs are considered a higher risk than general contractor continuing education or organic rose gardening seminars because customers for the former historically tend toward chargebacks, says Brian K. Roemmele of merchant bank 1st American Card Service in Murrieta, California. About 30 to 45 days after the seminar, these get-rich-quick hopers (or their irate spouses) often call their credit card company and demand their money back, claiming they didn't learn anything, which means the merchant card company charges you more in discount fees to compensate for the loss.

If you've got a stellar personal credit rating, your new company will probably pay a lower discount rate than someone who's had credit problems, although not all banks penalize the credit-deficient.

There are also all sorts of add-on fees to take into consideration. Take a look at the chart on page 49 to get an idea of what you'll pay for and how much.

Market Research

As we've explored, the amount you'll pay for market research is a variable, almost entirely dependent upon you, your personal style, and how comfortable you are with the topics you've chosen. If you're going to be selling workshops on how to write a winning romance novel to romance writers' groups, you know every would-be bodice-ripping author in five states, and you absolutely know they'll go for the topics you'll be offering, you can cut your market research expenses down to nearly nothing. If, on the other hand, you're not sure there's a market for your hydroponic broccoli seminars, nor how saleable they are, you have a lot of research ahead of you.

Merchant Account Fees

Item	Fees (Swiped*)	Fees (Mail, Phone, or Internet Order)
Discount rate (multiply each transaction by this rate, i.e., $200 ticket fee x 1.49% = $2.98 that the bank charges you to process the transaction)	1.49% to 1.61%	2.17% to 2.29%
Transaction fee (another fee the bank adds on for each transaction processed)	$.20 to $.25	$.25 to $.30
Monthly statement fee	$10	$10
Monthly minimum (if your total discount rate charges per month come to less than the monthly minimum, you must pay the difference; i.e., if your monthly minimum is $20 and your discount rate charges add up to $15, youll pay the whole $20)	$20 to $25	$20 to $25
Application fee	$0 to $75	$0 to $75
Programming fee	usually free with equipment lease or purchase	usually free with equipment lease or purchase
Electronic card terminal	$200 to $1,000 purchase or $16 to $73/month lease option	

*Merchant card services charge higher discount rates for orders taken by mail, internet, or phone than for those handled in person or swiped through the credit card terminal. Why? Because if a customer signs for your seminar or other product or service while he is standing there, you and the merchant service run less risk of a chargeback.

In addition to the fees shown here, you may be charged an AVS or address verification fee per transaction, a daily batchout fee to send charges from the electronic terminal to the merchant service in batches or chunks, and an annual "membership" fee. Be sure to ask—and negotiate—before you sign up!

Market Research Budget

Purchased mailing list of 3,000 names at $100 per 1,000 names	$300
3,000 brochure/questionnaires (two duplexed—printed on both sides—pages, black ink only), designed on your computer with your desktop-publishing program and copied by your local print shop	$360
Postage, 3,000 pieces at 26.8 cents each	$804
Standard or bulk mail permit (so you get the postage discount of 26.8 cents each instead of the usual 39 cents each)	$200
Telephone surveys, from genealogy society lists you already have, 100 calls at an average of $1.50 each	$150
Travel to genealogy conferences to conduct focus groups	$200
Total Market Research Budget	**$2,014**

So let's say you're somewhere in the middle. You're planning a series of seminars for genealogy buffs on writing their family histories. The chart above shows what your market research budget might look like. You will, of course, want to modify this budget to suit your own needs, but this should give you a good idea of how to start your own plan.

Phone Fun

We assume that you already have a telephone, in which case you already know all about phone bills. You should, however, install at least two separate, dedicated lines for your business. Costs, of course, depend on how many fun features you add to your telephone service and which local and long-distance carriers you go with, but for the purpose of start-up budgeting, let's say you should allocate $20 to $30 per line per month for basic service. You'll also need to add the phone company's installation fee, which should be in the range of $40 to $60. Check with your local phone company to determine exactly what these costs are in your area.

The Mechanical Receptionist

You won't always be available to answer your phone. So what, other than having the phone surgically attached to your ear, can you do? You've got two ways to go here: the trusty answering machine or the phone company's voice-mail service. For estimating start-up costs, let's figure a basic answering machine at about $15 and voice mail at about $12 to $18 per month, although—like everything else—your actual costs will depend on how many features you decide to add.

Top of the Charts

If you're unsure whether a merchant account that allows you to accept credit cards is right for your business, consider these 5 top reasons to do so, courtesy of merchant account and software provider Merchant Express:

1. *Increase sales.* Studies show businesses that accept credit cards can see a huge increase in volume.

2. *Legitimize your business.* Studies show that displaying credit card logos as forms of payment you accept creates a sense of trust, and when your customers trust you, they'll buy from you.

3. *Improve cash flow.* Funds from credit card sales are deposited into your bank account much faster than if you wait for checks to clear (on average 48 hours as opposed to seven or more days).

4. *Grab buyers.* Credit card holders buy more on impulse, are more affluent, and buy 2.5 times more merchandise than noncardholders.

5. *Increase order size.* On average, credit card holders tend to place larger orders than customers paying by cash or check. And customers paying by credit card tend to place extra orders and order more often.

My Calling Card

Company stationery is as important to your company image as a well-answered phone. Even though your customers may see only a web site or specially designed direct-mail piece, you'll still need stationery for your dealings with suppliers, corporate accounting departments, and bankers—the other, and also important, side of your business identity. To help build that solid, established identity—the one other businesses will want to work with—you'll need professional-quality letterhead, envelopes, and business cards.

You can purchase blank stationery, including cards, and print everything up yourself with a desktop-publishing program. Or you can have a set of stationery and business cards printed for you at a quick-print house like Kinko's or at Office Depot's inhouse service. Either way, you should allocate about $200 to $400, depending on how many you order (typically 500 to 1,000 each of letterhead, envelopes, and business cards) and the grade of paper and number of ink colors you choose.

Floating Pencils

You'll need pens, pencils, paper clips, a stapler, a letter opener, tape, and all-important printer cartridges. You'll also need blank paper for designing and printing direct-mail

Never Too Late

There's an element of debate surrounding the subject of extra-income products for the newbie. Many experts feel that spending a lot of money on BOR (back-of-the-room, remember?) goodies is suicidal for the start-up seminar entrepreneur. They counsel a resounding "no" on these items until you've got at least a couple of years—and a bit of working capital—under your cap and have made enough of a name for yourself to warrant promoting them.

Others feel that if you've got the start-up funds, you should go ahead and spring for BOR products on the grounds that they often produce as much income—or more—than the actual seminars.

So what's a seminar newbie to do? Your homework, for starters. If your market research and your experience in your niche field demonstrate that BOR products can make a sizable difference—and if you can afford them—go ahead and give them a try, keeping your costs and order quantities as low as possible. If you have any doubts, however, table the extra-income stuff for later in your career. It's never too late to produce them.

pieces, evaluation forms, workbooks, and invoices. If you figure that you're purchasing all of this brand new for the business (as if you didn't have scads of pens and pencils floating around the house), you can write in about $150.

Ticket to Ride

If you plan to hold public seminars, you'll want tickets. Just how many you'll need will depend upon how many attendees you expect. A law of printing services—whether you're running off tickets, evaluation forms or deeds to the first subdivision on the moon—is that the more you have printed, the less expensive it is per piece. If you start with 1,000 tear-off tickets, the kind where you keep the short stub and the attendee keeps the bigger portion, you can figure on spending about $100.

Work It Out

Workbooks are always a nice touch and in some programs, such as continuing education, they're a necessity. Again, your costs will depend upon your ultimate goal: You might want a simple outline so your participants feel they've got a little something to take home with them, or you might prefer a hard-core text in which people can work out problems or scribble notes during the program. As a rough guide, let's say you're putting together a 25-page booklet that will consist of single-sided bound pages. Five hundred spiral-bound copies will run you in the neighborhood of $1,450, while 500 copies of the same document stapled will cost about $550.

Back-of-the-Room Stuff

You can offer a wide range of back-of-the-room (BOR) products—from audios and videos and hardcover books to softcover pamphlets, prints, desktop toys, T-shirts, or whatever else might tie in with your programs. Besides video versions of your seminars, you will probably also want to invest in some short (about ten minute) demo videos; speakers bureaus will insist on them before signing you on, and so will many prospective clients.

Action, Camera!

Cutting your first demo or full-length video is exciting—you're a movie star! But before you get too star-struck, get real and consider all your options:

- *Do you want to go with VHS or DVD format?* While some professional videographers insist that "VHS is dead," many professional speakers still rely on it for demos. "Remember that the clients are watching at work," Gail Hahn in Reston, Virginia, advises, "and many clients' workplaces—especially government places—have not upgraded their equipment to DVD. Right now I offer both to clients and bureaus and ask them which they prefer. Some would rather watch on their computers, some would rather watch on a big-screen TV, and some only have a VCR. I have about half and half for requests."

    Dr. Jerry Old in Shawnee, Kansas, adds, "I'm still getting rid of my videotapes but plan to convert to DVDs soon. They'll be easier [and less expensive] to mail."

- *Do you want to go with an in-studio setup or have the production company shoot you live! during an actual presentation?* Some companies charge more to come to your event, while others charge more for studio taping. Studio taping gives you a chance to fine tune your performance and often produces a more polished soundtrack, but it'll cost more because

Bright Idea

Get creative with your video production contract. Some companies will give you the tapes for free if you give them a portion of your sales. This is a good way to get up and running with a video even if you don't have the funds for production. Make sure, though, that there's a cap on the number of copies sold whose profits you'll share.

you'll invariably spend more time stopping, starting, and generally fiddling to get everything perfect.

- *Do you want fancy titles, graphics, voice-over introductions, and music cues?* These frills can add oomph to your final product but will cost more as well.

- *Do you want to shave costs by designing and printing your own labels and hunting for packaging?* Production companies often charge extra for fancy labels or even for jewel cases and clamshells (the boxes DVDs and videotapes, respectively, come packaged in).

Beware!

If you plan to tape one of your seminars or workshops and you include participants in the footage, be sure to have them sign a release giving you permission to use them in your film.

Costs for producing audios and videos, whether on DVD or VHS, can vary considerably depending on the production company, the part of the country you're in, and the number of frills you choose. We've provided a sample pricing chart on page 55, but you need to do your own homework: Shop around, ask lots of questions, get references, ask to see samples, and then choose the studio with features and pricing you can live with.

Audio Excitement

Seminar attendees can be big consumers of audio CDs of your programs or of additional material that covers the same theme, so cutting that hit CD is worth considering. "Right now, I have a CD burner, a color printer, and a label maker, and I'm attempting to make smaller quantities of several different titles and do a print-on-demand system inhouse," Reston, Virginia, speaker Gail Hahn says. "I just purchased a digital voice recorder and will download my programs or radio talk shows or just me recording a session or reading my book into the recorder and then make an audio CD from it directly. Then I won't be stuck with inventory that isn't selling."

Stat Fact

In a recent survey by the National Speakers Association, the vast majority of respondents, 57.5 percent, said they spend between zero and $500 per year on video production. The next highest percentage, 17.1 percent, spends $501 to $1,000 per year, and only 2.3 percent claimed to spend between $3,001 and $5,000 per year on video production.

Author, Author

If you're already the bestselling author of *Night Golfing for Vampires*, you can buy copies of your work from the publisher, usually at 50 percent of the cover price, and offer them as part of

Sample Pricing Chart

	CD	DVD	VHS
Production	$50 to $100 per hour base rate[1]	$70 to $100 per hour base rate[2]	$70 to $100 per hour base rate[3]
Editing	$50 to $100 per hour	$50 to $100 per hour	$50 to $100 per hour
Reproduction 50 to 100 copies	$4 to $5 each, including jewel case[4]	$10 to $12 each, including jewel case[5]	$4 to $7 each, including sleeve and/or case[6]

1. You may incur extra charges depending on whether you record in the studio or on location, if you go with professional intros, outros or music cues, and/or titles or graphics. Some production facilities may also add on various studio or lab fees; be sure to ask before signing a contract.
2. Same as footnote 1 above. Also expect to pay a two-hour minimum.
3. Same as footnote 1 above. Also expect to pay a two-hour minimum.
4. You may incur extra charges for various graphics and printing options, depending on whether you provide your own artwork or have it done by the production facility, whether you go with printed inserts and type of case or cover you choose. Also expect to pay a setup fee of $10 to $50.
5. Same as footnote 4 above; you may find prices as low as $3 per unit if you do your own labeling and packaging.
6. Same as footnote 4 above. Price is for a 60-minute tape; costs increase or decrease commensurate with length.

your back-of-the-room cache. But if you don't yet have a book, you may want to figure the cost to produce one into your budget.

You can go a couple of different routes here: You can go with a vanity publisher, in which case you don't get royalties or advances like you would if you were Stephen King or Danielle Steele, but you don't run any risk of rejection, either. Instead, you pay a flat fee and the publisher obtains an ISBN (International Standard Book Number, necessary for cataloging by libraries, booksellers, and distributors), has your manuscript edited, has the cover and any graphics designed and executed, and then, of course,

Bright Idea

Design your own cover using your trusty desktop-publishing program (at a cost of zero!) or have an artistic friend make one up for you in exchange for babysitting, dinner on the town, or an artistic credit on your tapes.

Audiotape Production Costs

	One 1-Hour Tape	Album of Six 1-Hour Tapes
Cutting the master tape(s): recording and editing	$200 + $250 to $500 for extras like voice-over intros and music library clips	$1,500 + $250 to $500 for extras like voice-over intros and music library clips
Duplicating 100 copies in poly boxes	$ .90/copy + $150 to $300 for imprinting title and other info on cassette*	$8.50/copy + $150 to $300 for imprinting title and other info on cassette*
Duping 500 copies in poly boxes	$ .75/copy + $150 to $300 for imprinting title and other info on cassette*	$7.95/copy + $150 to $300 for imprinting title and other info on cassette*
Duping 1,000 copies in poly boxes	$ .60/copy + $150 to $300 for imprinting title and other info on cassette*	$6.95/copy + $150 to $300 for imprinting title and other info on cassette*

Add on a one-time $25 fee to create plates for imprinting your tapes.

Don't forget that you'll want artwork for your J-cards or album covers. Some studios will handle the printing for you; at others, it's up to you.

has the book printed. Hahn went this route and tallied her costs at about $3,000 for 1,000 copies of a pocket-sized volume that's roughly 3½ inches by 4¼ inches.

Or you can go with a commercial printer that specializes in books. Costs to go this route vary with the size of your book, whether you want a hard or soft cover, how fancy you get with colors and graphics, and how many copies you order. As a rough guide, you can expect to pay $3 to $5 per copy for 1,000 copies (amounts smaller than this may not be cost effective). Keep in mind, however, that you'll have other costs to consider as well, such as ISBNs (purchased in blocks of ten or more at a beginning cost of $250), artwork, typesetting and copy editing. For more information on all this and more, check out Entrepreneur's *Start Your Own Self-Publishing Business*.

> ## Seminar Speak
> When discussing book prices with your printer, you'll want to ask for perfect binding. This refers not to the caliber of the work, which, of course, should be perfect, but to the way paperback books are normally bound—as opposed to being stapled or spiral-bound.

Sign of the Times

You may want signs to point out your registration table and your back-of-the-room products table, and to direct customers to other areas like autographing and workbooks or other handouts. Pencil in about $75 for a collection of signs that can be used again and again, provided you don't let the kids use them as sleds.

Shipping Supplies

If you plan to offer BOR products, you'll need a few shipping and packaging supplies so that you can mail out all those goodies that people decide they just have to have after they get home. As a start-up figure, pencil in about $100.

All That Jazz

Other expenses you'll need to plug into your start-up expense chart are business licenses, business insurance, legal advice, utility deposits, and all that jazz—the costs intrinsic to any company's inception. Use the worksheet on page 62 to pencil in and then tally up these costs and all the others we've discussed in this section. If you copy a couple of extra sheets, you can work up several options, compare them all and decide which will work the best for you to arrive at your Official Start-Up Figure.

Figuring Profits

Now that we've determined how much it's going to cost you to get your business up and running, let's turn to the fun part—figuring out how much you can expect to make. Which, of course, means figuring out how to price your services.

Warning: This section contains actual math problems. If you're one of us arithmetic phobic types, you may be tempted at this point to take this book and toss it out the window. Don't! There's a big difference between having to calculate when two trains traveling

Gems or Junk?

I f you decide to offer a selection of goodies for the seminar set— things likeT-shirts emblazoned with "Vampire Golf: Sink Your Teeth Into It," coffee mugs with inspirational sayings or stress-buster pencils that double as pacifiers—you'll find that your costs will depend entirely upon what you'll sell.

When you think BOR products, think cautiously. If you hit on the right formula of "toys" for your programs, they can potentially add hundreds of dollars to your monthly income. But if not, the alternative is a collection of tchotchkes you may have a hard time unloading, even at a yard sale.

at different speeds on the same track will meet, and figuring out how much money you can actually make in your own seminar business, which is fun! So sit back and enjoy.

Public Seminar Pricing

To determine how much you'll make, you have to figure out how much to charge for your programs, and the best way to do that is to first figure out how much each seminar will cost you. Let's give you yet another incarnation and say you're going to do a workshop on "Living the Good Life with Your Own Bed-and-Breakfast Business." This will be a public program at a swanky downtown hotel and, based on your market research, you're expecting about 100 attendees. Take a look at the chart on page 59 to get an idea what your costs to present this one seminar will be.

OK, we have come up with a cost per seminar of $2,000. Now let's figure out how much tickets will have to go for in order to make the seminar pay for itself. That's easy: Divide your cost of $2,000 by the 100 people you expect to attend. You get a ticket price of $20. But keep in mind that this is your break-even price. If you sell tickets for $20 each, you won't make a dime.

If you double your ticket price to $40, you'll make a gross profit of $4,000, which sounds pretty good! That is, if your prospective customers will pay this much for your seminar and if they all show up. Your market research should clue you in to whether or not this is a viable price.

Dollar Stretcher

Don't forget that you can add considerably to your profits with back-of-the-room sales. If you sell $1,000 worth of products that cost you $500, you've just made $500!

Seminar Production Costs

Living the Good Life with Your Own Bed-and-Breakfast Business	
Item	Cost per Seminar
Site	$350
Refreshments	50
Workbooks	500
Two employees (to work registration desk and product table)	100
Advertising and promotion	1,000
Total	**$2,000**

The Mad Scientist

If it's not, you'll have to go back to the drawing board and—like a good mad scientist—rework your calculations. Either lower your ticket price, say to $30, which will give you a gross profit per seminar of $1,000 (your $2,000 costs subtracted from your $3,000 ticket sales), or figure out how to lower your costs, for example, by negotiating a better site rental rate, cutting down on the refreshments, or going with less expensive workbooks.

Now let's say you've got it down to $30 per ticket, 100 people per seminar, and a gross profit of $1,000, plus that extra $500 in back-of-the-room sales, which means you're grossing $1,500 per seminar. If you do 24 of these seminars a year, or two a month, you'll gross $36,000.

You'll also need to consider whether there's a market for your bed-and-breakfast seminars within reasonable driving distance of your home base 50 weeks a year. If not, you'll either have to add travel costs for taking your show on the road—which will put a major dent in your bottom line—or you'll have to design a series of programs (like starting your own bed-and-breakfast, starting your own coffee bar, starting

Stat Fact
According to a recent survey by the National Speakers Association, 22.9 percent of respondents received an average of $3,001 to $5,000 for a keynote/general session speech, 17.6 percent of respondents received an average of $2,001 to $3,000 for a breakout session, and 19.9 percent received the same average of $2,001 to $3,000 for a training session.

your own personal concierge service, starting your own wax museum, etc.). This way you don't exhaust your customer base.

Private Seminar Pricing

Another way to go is with private seminars, in which the client—the corporation or association—pays all your travel expenses, including lodging and meals. Let's say you're doing seminars for credit card companies' customer service representatives on "Keeping Customers on Hold Forever the Cheerful Way," and you're going to charge $3,000 per full-day session. If you do two seminars a month, you're grossing $6,000 per month, and you can take your show all over the country—or even the world—without worrying about travel expenses.

Private, or corporate, seminar pricing is entirely different from public seminar pricing. Denise Dudley's Mission, Kansas, company, SkillPath, for instance, charges $99 to $299 for public seminars, while its corporate programs range from $2,000 to $3,000 and up—or $7,000 to $8,000 for seminars where they supply the computers on which participants train.

However you go, private or public, your gross revenue is not the whole story, because you'll have more expenses than just those for each seminar. Which brings us to . . . drum roll, please . . .

Operating Expenses

These are the various and sundry costs that make up the backbone of every seminar professional's operation. Subtracted from your projected gross profits, these operating expenses will tell the true tale of how much you'll be making. Ready? Here we go:

We're going to assume once again that you'll be homebased, so we won't worry about expenses for office rent or utilities. But we do need to consider the following:

- phone
- postage
- web hosting (so your web site, if you choose to have one, has a server to keep it up and running)
- electronic credit card processing
- stationery and office supplies
- ISP
- loan repayment

> **Smart Tip** _Tip..._
> Your customers, as well as many of your vendors, will expect you to have a fax machine for sending and receiving orders, invoices, and a wide variety of other materials. Purchase a fax machine for $100 to $350 (or more), depending on features.

The Financial Perspective

"**F**rom a purely financial perspective," Larry Smith of Omaha, Nebraska-based National Electrical Seminars says, "a two-day public seminar with 100 participants at $159 each is wonderful. I average 100 to 150 training days a year. Our fee for public seminars is $110 per participant for a one-day seminar and $159 for the two-day seminars. After some investigation, we found this to be a competitive rate for the Midwest, which is where most of our seminars are.

"My favorite audience," he adds, "is made up largely of repeat participants. The time interval might be one or two, and sometimes three years. Participants get excited about attending our seminars and come energized and ready to learn. There might actually have been a few seminars where the participants picked me up. I might have been tired from traveling or not feeling good—it's hard to ignore their enthusiasm."

Phone (From) Home

As we discussed in the start-up section of this chapter, phone service is a must in the seminar business. Start with a base rate of $25 per line per month—one for your business, which is separate from your home phone, and one for your fax machine and e-mail. Then add in estimated long-distance charges based on where your clients and customers will be located, how often you expect to call them, and what sort of rate you've negotiated with your long-distance carrier. If you plan to do public seminars in various regions around the country, you may want to invest in a toll-free number so customers can call you at your cost instead of theirs. Rates for toll-free numbers range from 3 cents per minute to 8 cents per minute, plus service fees of $10 to $48 per month (generally based on the number of incoming calls), but if the number of customers you'll attract increases exponentially, it may be worth it.

Dollar Stretcher

Be environmentally and economically smart. Reuse that printer paper. Instead of practicing hoop shots into the trash with all those versions of letters, evaluation sheets, and other printed materials that you decided you didn't like, set the pages aside. When you've compiled a tidy stack, load them back into your printer and print on the blank side. Save your "good" paper for the final draft that goes out in the mail.

Start-Up Costs

Costs	TravelTeach	So Romantic
Rent		$1,200
Office expenses (equipment, software, furniture, and supplies—see charts in Chapter 7 starting on page 121)	$3,744	9,323
Market research		2,114
Electronic credit card processing	200	1,000
Licenses	150	150
Bulk-mail permit		300
Phone	100	360
Utility deposits		150
Employee payroll		3,500
Grand opening	100	500
Legal services	375	525
Miscellaneous postage	60	120
Internet service provider	22	50
Web site design and marketing		500
Insurance	500	600
Inventory		2,500
Miscellaneous expenses (add roughly 10% of total)	525	2,289
Total Start-Up Costs	**$5,776**	**$25,181**

Start-Up Costs Worksheet

Costs	
Rent	$
Office expenses (equipment, software, furniture, and supplies	
Market research	
Electronic credit card processing	
Licenses	
Bulk-mail permit	
Phone	
Utility deposits	
Employee payroll	
Grand opening	
Legal services	
Miscellaneous postage	
Internet service provider	
Web site design and marketing	
Insurance	
Inventory	
Miscellaneous expenses (add roughly 10% of total)	
Total Start-Up Costs	$

Bloomin' Postage

As your company grows, your postage expenses will bloom, too, but for your first year of operation you should be able to keep them to a minimum. If you figure on an average of two pieces of mail per day at the good old first-class rate of 39 cents per piece, you can pencil in $22 per month.

Web Host

If you've got a web site, you'll need a web host, which is not a dapper chap in a tuxedo standing at the door with a tray of champagne cocktails, but the computer or computers that handle all your customer traffic. A web host can be likened to an ISP like AOL or CompuServe. While you can manipulate your web site all you want from your home/office computer, it takes a much, much larger server to handle the complexities and volume of web traffic, and that's why you need a host. How much can you expect to pay? In the range of $20 to $50 per month.

Smart Tip

Tip...

Peek into the U.S. Postal Service web site at www.usps.com. It's got lots of nifty features including a postage rate calculator, business-mail and direct-mail tutorials, and online printing and mailing services.

The Armchair Seminar

For the armchair presenter or audience, a new permutation of seminars is evolving: the web seminar (or webinar). In this version of virtual reality, programs are presented online, complete—with some technologies—with PowerPoint presentations, audio and video interaction with attendees (who can virtually raise their hands to be recognized), and an assortment of other bells and whistles that emulate live programs.

Buying your own webinar software is very expensive; the best way to go is to contract with a web conferencing service, such as Genesys Conferencing or WebEx. You schedule your seminar with the company, upload your slides or other graphics to them, and they do all the techie stuff that makes your webinar work. Web conferencing services generally charge either a subscription fee ranging from $75 to $750 per month, depending on the number of "seats" and length of program, or on a pay-as-you-go basis that ranges from 33 cents to 45 cents per minute per participant.

Getting Carded

To keep your merchant card service humming along, you'll pay a monthly statement fee of about $10. And if you've decided to lease your terminal instead of purchase it, you'll have that fee of $16 to $73 per month to account for as well.

Paper Tiger

Once you've made your initial outlay for office supplies and stationery, your fixed expenses in this category should be fairly low. Staples last a long time, and you can reuse paper clips.

Your main expense will be paper: paper for your printer and fax machine, fine-quality paper for stationery, and envelopes. You can refer to the sample office expenses chart on page 123 in Chapter 7 for prices.

Olé! Online Service

What praises have we not already sung for the ISP? As we've said (repeatedly), this is a must service for the seminar production professional. It's also, in most cases, a fixed expense. ISPs generally charge a flat rate of $20 to $25 for unlimited monthly service, which gives you access to the World Wide Web and to e-mail.

Paying the Piper

We've set aside a fixed expense called loan repayment. If you don't borrow money to start your business, you won't need to bother with this one. If, however, you finance your start-up costs through any means, you'll need to repay the piper. Here's where you pencil in whatever your monthly fee is.

Putting It Together

You can use the worksheet on page 66 to pencil in your projected income and estimated operating expenses. You may have many more expenses than the ones discussed here, such as employees and the workers' compensation and payroll costs that go with them, auto expenses, subscription fees for professional publications, butler and maid service (just dreaming!), and pizza delivery or Chinese take-out costs. We've included rent, utilities, employee and insurance costs on our worksheet because they're a common feature of financial projections, and you should be familiar with them. If they don't apply to your company, of course, you won't need to worry about them.

Once you've calculated your estimated operating expenses, you can subtract them from your calculated earnings and—voilà!—you have a projected income/expense total.

Projected Income/Operating Expenses Statements

	TravelTeach	So Romantic
Projected monthly income:	$1,667	$16,675
Projected monthly operating expenses:		
Rent		1,200
Phone/utilities	75	1,175
Credit card processing (electronic terminal)	20	45
Employee payroll		3,500
Miscellaneous postage	20	500
Insurance	90	90
Web hosting	30	85
Miscellaneous expenses (stationery/office supplies)	10	50
Shipping and packing materials		100
Loan repayment		200
Internet service provider	22	50
Total expenses	267	6,995
Projected Net Monthly Income	$1,400	$9,680

Projected Income/Operating Expenses Worksheet

Projected monthly income: $_____

Projected monthly operating expenses:

Rent $_____

Phone/utilities   _____

Credit card processing
(electronic terminal)   _____

Employee payroll   _____

Miscellaneous postage   _____

Insurance   _____

Web hosting   _____

Miscellaneous expenses
(stationery and office supplies)   _____

Shipping and packing materials   _____

Loan repayment   _____

Internet service provider   _____

Total expenses: $_____

Projected Net Monthly Income $_____

Romancing the Bank

Now that you have done all the arithmetic, you can determine just how much you will need to get your business up and running. And as a bonus, you can show all these beautifully executed figures to your lender to show him or her that your business is a good risk and that you will be able to repay the loan without difficulty.

You might want to consider financing through your bank or credit union. In this case, your start-up cost and income figures are very important. The bank will want to see all of this, neatly laid out and carefully calculated. You'll also want to show them all the statistics you can gather—for instance, the ones in this book—about the bright future of the seminar industry.

Gail Hahn opened a $5,000 line of credit at her bank as a backup in case of cash flow problems but found she didn't need it. "I was completely self-funded from my savings and investments," she says proudly. "I repaid my loan to myself in the second year of business."

In Your Pocket

Most entrepreneurs use a very exclusive source to finance their start-up expenses—family and friends. You may choose to go this route yourself. You'll have a lot less paperwork to fill out, and you can let your financier share in the excitement as your business takes off. But remember that you'll still need to figure the repayment of borrowed funds into your costs and that you should treat your repayment agreement as seriously as you would any bank loan.

Another route many entrepreneurs take to obtain financing is through an entity as close as your back pocket—the credit card. Before you choose this option, take a look at your available credit balance and—important—at the annual percentage rate. Card companies frequently offer low, low rates as an incentive to sign up. Go with the one that offers the best rate for the longest period of time.

> **Bright Idea**
> To make the best possible impression on your banker, assemble your start-up materials in a professional-looking folder along with your desktop-published brochure or price lists. The more businesslike your company looks, the better.

Behind the Podium
Daily Operations

y this time, you're probably wondering what exactly a seminar professional does all day. Spend a few hours with a mike in your hand, wowing your audience with your wit and brilliance, and then sit back and sign autographs? Spend all day selling BOR (back-of-the-room) stuff hoping your participants don't think you're a giant bore?

The reality is yes to both of these scenarios—plus a whole lot more. In this chapter, we take a peek behind the podium at the daily life of a seminar professional and explore the ins and outs of seminar operations.

Seminar Countdown

Like baking cookies, hosting a sit-down dinner for 12 or adding a new bathroom to your house, when you produce a seminar, you need to plan ahead. If you're doing private seminars where the client plans the conference or convention and makes all the arrangements, you can skate through a good portion of this countdown. (This doesn't mean skip this part—you'll still find lots of valuable tips!) But if you'll do public seminars where it's up to you to make all the arrangements, heads up!

Unlike those sit-down dinner schedules they print in ladies' magazines that tell you to pick up the roast moose from the market three days ahead of time, then bake and freeze your gooseberry tartlets two days ahead of time, there's no one set-in-concrete time frame for planning a seminar. It's wise to start planning as early as possible—ideally four to six months before your program. But it all depends on a lot of variables. Take a look at the "Seminar Countdown Worksheet" starting on page 71 and then follow along with us.

Countdown Item 1
Get with the Program

One of your most important tasks as a seminar professional will be to design your program—if you haven't got a seminar, you're not going to get very far! You did a lot of the design work when you did your market research, choosing your target market and narrowing down your niche to the one that best suits both your audience and you. Now it's time to get down to specifics, like who will present your programs, how long they'll last and where you'll hold them. So let's get going!

Now Presenting

Will you present the seminars yourself or hire speakers? If you choose the latter, you'll need to decide whether you'll turn them loose to do their own thing or design a curriculum that everybody follows. This is an important consideration. If you choose your speakers based on their special stories, insights, and personalities, there's no point in tampering with success. That would be like hiring Mick Jagger for a concert and instructing him to sing Perry Como hits.

Seminar Countdown Worksheet

Write your decisions in the spaces provided; then check off a task well done.

Item 1 (usually four months ahead):

❑ Choose presenters (if other than yourself): _____

_____

❑ Start writing and designing workbooks or handouts.

❑ Choose program format (e.g., half-day seminar, two-day workshop): ____

_____

❑ Decide on program times (e.g., Saturday 9 A.M. to noon, or Tuesday through Thursday, 9 A.M. to noon and 2 P.M. to 4:30 P.M.): _____

_____

❑ Choose dream dates: _____

❑ Decide on city or resort area: _____

❑ Choose hotel, conference center, or other site: _____

❑ Choose food or beverages and order from hotel: _____

_____

❑ Choose meals (if any) and order from hotel: _____

_____

❑ Place orders for:

__ Signs from hotel/printer (circle one)

__ Video equipment from hotel/vendor (circle one)

__ Microphone from hotel

__ Podium from hotel

❑ Send confirmation/contract request letter to hotel.

❑ Choose a seating plan:_____

Item 2 (usually three months ahead):

❑ Finalize your ticket or enrollment price: _____

❑ Design sales materials.

❑ Negotiate printing price for sales materials; order from printer.

❑ Pick up sales materials from printer.

❑ Put together magazine press kits and mail to: _____

_____

❑ Send sales materials to:_____

Seminar Countdown Worksheet, continued

❑ If you'll use salespeople, send them out to call on: _____

_____

Item 3 (usually two months ahead):
❑ Finalize workbooks and other handouts.
❑ Place orders for:
__ Audio duping
__ Video duping
__ Books from printer/publisher (circle one)
__ Other *(List what was ordered and how many of each.)*

_____

❑ Order workbooks, evaluation forms, agendas, and other handouts from
printer. *(List what was ordered and how many of each.)*

_____

❑ Make travel arrangements for yourself, your assistants, speakers, or presenters:

_____

_____

❑ Send press kits to newspapers.

Item 4 (one week before):
❑ Contact hotel with attendance count and confirm arrangements.

Item 5 (two days before):
❑ Call hotel with final head count and final confirmation of arrangements.

Item 6 (the day before):
❑ Familiarize yourself with room layout and facilities.
❑ Check that all site-provided equipment is present and in working order.
❑ Check seating arrangements.
❑ Check room temperature.
❑ Go over battle plans with assistants.

Item 7 (the big day):
❑ Check room setup again.
❑ Check equipment again.
❑ Set up tables for registration, handouts, and products.
❑ Set up credit card terminal.
❑ Remove any ashtrays and set out no-smoking signs.

But if you are developing a standardized program, for example a customer service course for bank employees, then you might want to hire several trainers whom you can send to or base in various parts of the country and have all your trainers give the exact same workshop. This way, your clients—the corporations who will hire you—are assured that every employee in every branch office receives the same material and the same presentation.

Smart Tip

Tip...

"Start with one seminar," SkillPath Seminars' Denise Dudley recommends. "Then spin off and plan the next one. Plan two for the next month, then three the next— get your momentum going."

Work on Those Workbooks

Decide on any workbooks or other handouts you'll want to include with your seminar and start writing and designing them. You don't have to have a college textbook-sized tome—or anything at all if you feel it's not necessary—but remember that people like to have something to take away with them. And if that something has your name and contact information on it, it will help them remember you and enroll again.

Packaging Time

You'll also need to decide how long your program will run. Do you have enough material to keep your participants interested over the course of a two-day workshop? Or will a two-hour seminar be enough?

Break Time!

Build adequate breaks into your program. Everybody needs time to stand up, stretch their legs and their brains, primp in the restroom and make those important phone calls that can't wait until they get back to the real world. People tend to get antsy if they don't get a break every couple of hours; a break also gives you time to regroup, stretch, and run to the restroom.

Lunch breaks should be at least an hour in length, but can be stretched to one and a half or even two hours without fear that your audience will get lost and not come back. Make sure, however, that you've got something enticing planned and announced for the after-lunch period. This way you don't run the risk of participants deciding they've already heard the "good" part of your program and sneaking off to the pool bar.

Once you know how much time to allot, you'll need to decide how to package it. For instance, if you're planning a two-day workshop, you can arrange two sessions of equal length, say 10 A.M. to 4 P.M. each. Or you can cram most of your material into a long first day that runs from 9 A.M. to 4 or 5 P.M. and then make the second session more leisurely, say 11 A.M. to 3 P.M. or 9 A.M. to noon. You might choose this option for a weekend program, so people work hard on Saturday and then have Sunday as a sort of kick-back, discuss-what's-

Bright Idea

Try scheduling your seminar right before or after your target audience's national shindig—people who'll be in town to attend the meeting can attend your event without adding extra travel expenses or significantly more time away from work.

been-learned day. This format might be appealing to participants who've come from out of town and need Sunday to get back on the road, or for people at a weeklong convention or conference who might want to take the latter half of the second day to sightsee or play with the kids in the pool.

Dream Dates

Choose your dream dates. These are not Julia Roberts or Antonio Banderas, but days that your prospective audience will perceive as swell times for attending a seminar. You might schedule a beauty makeover program for women during Super Bowl weekend, but a dress-for-success seminar for men during the same weekend would totally bomb. Make sure you take the following into consideration when planning a seminar:

- *Holiday havoc.* If your program falls too close to the winter holidays, your customers may not go for it. People spend a lot of time with family, travel, attend parties, and do lots of planning during this time, and they won't want to tear themselves away from the fun for your program. Or they might reserve a ticket months early, but when it comes time to attend your seminar, they decide they've spent too much on holiday gift-giving and back out at the last minute. And if they've prepaid by credit card, you get hit with chargebacks, which is not good for your bottom line. (Remember this from Chapter 4?)

- *Event horizons.* Think about what other events may interfere with your plans. If you schedule your seminar dangerously close on the calendar to the World Series, Easter, a national election, or a biggie regional event like the Indian Summer Seafood Festival or Mardi Gras, your prospective participants might decide these affairs are more of a can't-miss than your program.

- *Convention chaos.* Think about the red-letter events on your particular audience's calendar. If your target audience is artists, crafters and gift merchandise retailers, don't plan your workshop for the same weeks as major gift shows. If your potential

Take a Seat

While you're making time and format decisions, you should also develop your seating arrangements. Just like Miss Morgenstern did in your first-grade classroom, you'll find that different seating patterns work best for different formats. Programs big on participation and interaction need more eye contact among attendees than those that are strictly listen-and-learn. "Participants need to be broken down into small study groups," advises Larry Smith of National Electrical Seminars in Omaha, Nebraska. "Working in small groups of five facilitates training and gives the group a sense of community. The smaller the group, the more interactive activities are possible. Interactive participant-centered training maximizes retention."

Audience size is also a factor—and one that you'll need to confirm with the hotel or conference center. Check out "Seating for Success" on page 95 for arrangement ideas.

participants are high school teachers, don't schedule your seminar during finals when your audience will want to be at their posts, looming over students. And if you're aiming for attorneys, don't plan your gig at the same time as the American Bar Association convention. Otherwise, all those lawyers will be living it up in, say, Chicago, while you're sitting all alone in Sheboygan with your seminar materials and no audience. The only exception to this rule is, of course, if you can get your program listed as one of the official convention events. In that case, you've got a captive audience!

- *Weather wrinkles.* In some parts of the country, brutal weather can make a difference in attendance. People may well cancel their reservations—or not show up for at-the-door sales—during blizzard conditions in the Midwest or Northeast. And people along the Gulf and Atlantic coasts won't show for your seminar—no matter how stellar—if a hurricane's lurking offshore. You can't, of course, know precisely when these weather events will occur (if you can, you've got terrific seminar material!), but you can avoid scheduling programs during the winter season or summer hurricane season in affected areas.

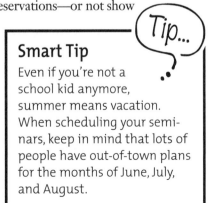

Smart Tip

Even if you're not a school kid anymore, summer means vacation. When scheduling your seminars, keep in mind that lots of people have out-of-town plans for the months of June, July, and August.

- *Days of the week.* Depending on your seminar, some days are better than others. Check out the chart on page 89 for a list of pros and cons for each day of the week.

Check out the chart on page 89

Smart Tip
Some hotels and conference centers provide shuttle service from airports. This is a plus worth mentioning in your sales materials.

A Different Crowd

After deciding when you'll have your seminar, don't forget the all-important decision as to where you'll host it. Your choices can range from a community center to a ballroom at the Ritz. Naturally, one's going to be pricier than the other, but one will also draw a different crowd than the other. So how do you choose?

First, realize that—as we explained in Chapter 4—your site price will be built into your ticket price, so you're not actually "paying" for the hotel or conference site all on your own, although you will have to pay an upfront deposit before you've garnered all your ticket sales.

The Hotel Booking Puzzle

Denise Dudley of SkillPath Seminars in Mission, Kansas, suggests booking hotels four months ahead and starting your advertising two months ahead of the seminar. Hotel booking, she says, is like working out a puzzle. Say you plan to schedule contiguous programs in Chicago, Milwaukee, and Madison—one each on Tuesday, Wednesday, and Thursday. You successfully reserve meeting rooms in the first two but discover that every room in Madison is booked solid. So now you have to go back and rework your "puzzle" to make the pieces fit, maybe making Madison the first stop and Chicago the last.

And that, Denise points out, is why you don't want to wait until the last minute to make your reservations.

National Electrical Seminars' Larry Smith has a similar method for dealing with hotel booking madness. "We make a list of cities that we want to schedule a seminar in," says the Omaha, Nebraska, entrepreneur. "Then we make a list of our available dates. We then begin to call hotels looking for available dates. The availability of the meeting room usually dictates when we schedule the seminar in a given city. It is during this process that we use our meeting planner form. [See page 92.] So the hotel reservations are made in the very beginning of the process."

But even if you build your hotel facility into the cost of your tickets, you've still got a lot of decisions to make: Do you go with the hotel that's a downtown dowager or with one that's new and classy but out in the 'burbs? Do you forgo the traditional hotel altogether and choose a conference center that's out in the country? Or do you go with the community center?

Take a look at these tips for making the right decision:

- *Compatibility.* Choose a site that's a good match with your participants and your subject matter. If you're doing a program for business executives, you might choose a snazzy, modern hotel near the airport or in a fashionable, upscale semi-burb like Beverly Hills or Buckhead because these are the types of environments where the suit crowd feels comfortable (and considers worth its time and money). If, on the other hand, your seminar subject is the paranormal, you might seek out an old downtown hotel with an ambience of emanations and possibly even a resident ghost or two. One more either/or example: If your topic is "Landscape Instead Of Lawn" and your participants will be seniors or stay-at-home moms, a community room in the park might be the perfect place. But if your topic is "Landscape Instead of Lawn" and your participants are professional landscape architects on a two-day workshop, a conference center in an upscale resort area would be more the thing.

- *Location, location.* Will your participants be arriving by plane, train or automobile? If you'll have lots of travelers arriving from out-of-town, you'll want a site that's easily accessible from airports and interstates. If people will be coming from across town instead of across the country, choose a location that's freeway- or major thoroughfare-close, doesn't require nerves of steel for traffic negotiations, and provides adequate (and not breathtakingly expensive) parking.

Coffee, Tea, or Brie

Decide whether you'll offer coffee, tea, or brie—or none of the above. Just as people always remember (usually unfavorably) what was served for supper on a plane trip, seminar participants take into vivid account the various "freebies" offered as part of the program package.

Even if your program only lasts a few hours, offer your attendees a choice of beverages: coffee, tea, soft drinks, or juices. Since everybody has a sweet tooth, a selection of sweet rolls or donuts for a morning program is always a nice touch. And some sort of afternoon goodie—brownies, cookies, or cake—is never unwelcome.

Since coffee and other beverages at a hotel can run from $3 to $7 per person, it's often more

Beware!
Even if you offer only water, the hotel will likely charge you for it, so if you're going to offer something, go for splashier treats than plain old H_2O.

cost-effective to offer a continental breakfast through the hotel. You get not only coffee, tea, and juice, but muffins, croissants, and other delectables for about the same price as coffee alone.

Smart Tip

"When you find a good hotel," seminar professional Larry Smith counsels, "continue to use it. Don't let price be the determining factor."

If your seminar lasts all day, you may decide to spring for lunch. Your participants will perceive this as a nice little bonus, even though in actuality you'll have added it into the cost of the ticket. This is definitely an optional item and one that's a source of considerable debate among seminar professionals. Some experts feel that price-included lunches or dinners are not really appreciated by participants—that the average attendee would rather fend for himself than have to make chitchat with his peers. Others believe the "free" lunch is a nice perk.

If you don't offer lunch, be sure there's a suitable restaurant on-site or nearby so your participants have time to eat before getting back to your program. If you live near the hotel or meeting site, have the facility give you a sample—you don't want people to remember your "free" lunch as an unappetizing rubber-chicken special.

Once you've made all your hotel-related decisions, send a letter to the sales or catering manager (whoever you've been dealing with) to confirm everything you've

Bad Rap 'Burgs

Your choice for where to hold your seminar is not relegated only to the hotel or other meeting site. You'll need to decide what city, 'burb or resort area you want. Your market research should tell you which ones will be better for your company based on the available population that will be interested in your programs and the economic levels that will allow those people to pay for your seminars. A "Surfing for Fun and Spirituality" workshop won't play in Peoria, where there's no surf, but would find a willing audience in Los Angeles.

Once you've made this sort of regional distinction, you need to narrow down your locale still further by choosing a specific city. Some 'burgs have a bad rap: People would rather attend a meeting in Beverly Hills or Irvine than in Watts or Garden Grove, even though they're all within the greater L.A. metropolitan area because the first two have a much safer and smarter (as in trendier) connotation, while the second two sound dangerous or dumpy. In New Jersey, say Trenton and Princeton and see which people choose!

hammered out and request a contract. Take a look at the sample hotel confirmation letter on page 90. When you receive the contract, you'll have some assurance that he or she has actually made the proper arrangements.

Don't forget that besides negotiating dates, times, eats, and drinks, you'll also want to work out the details on any equipment you'll want the hotel to provide, such as podiums, microphones, video monitors, and VCRs. If you'll work from a site like a community center that doesn't have these items and you'll need to order them from a vendor, you can do this now as well.

Countdown Item 2
Sales Products

After you've decided what food freebies you'll offer, you can finalize your ticket or enrollment price. Double-check it against your market research. Is it an appropriate fee for the benefits you're offering? How does it compare with competitors'

Sleep On It

Hotels have various departments set up to handle meetings, catered affairs, and banquets. So how do you know who to talk to, especially if you're also arranging for sleeping rooms for your out-of-town participants as well as yourself? "Most of the time the sales and catering [department] will handle the meeting room arrangements," advises Omaha, Nebraska, seminar provider Larry Smith. "We've learned not to let them make sleeping room arrangements. Reserve sleeping rooms yourself—sales and catering are not to be trusted with them."

Smith has not only gotten a handle on the sleeping room dilemma; he's designed a terrific technique for dealing with meeting room decisions. "To facilitate meeting arrangements," he says, "I developed a meeting planner form [see page 92]. We fill out the form on every event, follow up with a form letter explaining our expectations and needs, then wait for a meeting room contract.

"Go over the contract very carefully," Smith advises. "One week from the event we contact the sales and catering [department] to give them an approximate attendance count and talk over final arrangements. Two days before the event, we contact them again to give a final guaranteed count."

Send Out the Pep Squad

As soon as your sales materials are ready, pick them up and get going! This is when the promotion of your seminar really starts. If you'll use salespeople, send them out now to call on potential business clients. Do all you can to encourage preregistration. Try these tips:

- ○ Offer a discounted price (mark up sold-at-the-door tickets by 15 to 20 percent).
- ○ Assign seats in order of ticket purchase and say you do this in your brochure.
- ○ Offer even greater discounts for preregistered groups or students.
- ○ Give a $5 or $10 coupon off BOR products to those who preregister.

prices? Remember that even if you're offering pheasant under glass for luncheon as part of the price, people won't pay more than what they think the program is worth.

Now that you've got your enrollment price down, you can start to work on your sales products—brochures, letters, and advertisements. (We will explore how to develop these materials in Chapters 10 and 11.) Gather the elements you'll want—photos of yourself or your speakers if you'll be hiring out and copies of book covers, newspaper articles, testimonials from previous delighted participants, or other favorable blurbs. Design your sales materials, and then negotiate prices with printers, choose the best one, and place your print order.

Once your materials are printed and ready to go, put together press kits for magazines and send them out.

Countdown Item 3
Place Your Orders

Finalize the writing and design of any workbooks and place orders for signs and audiovisual equipment, either from the hotel or from private suppliers. Order your BOR products from vendors, audio and video duping services, and book sources (printer or publisher). By this time, you should have a good idea of how many participants to expect. Order workbooks, evaluation

Beware!

Take credit card information, but don't actually enter it into your electronic terminal until the day before the seminar. (Be sure to inform registrants that this is your company's policy.) This way, people who back out will probably have done so already and you avoid those nasty chargebacks.

First Class or Coach?

If you hire out big-name speakers—from astronauts and movie personalities to politicians and pop psychologists—you'll be the one to cover travel arrangements and costs. Know what they want and make sure you can provide it. Do they demand first class or are they good eggs who'll gladly go coach? What about hotel accommodations?

Keep in mind that many professionals on the lecture circuit have hectic schedules and may not know where they'll be the day before your program until two to four weeks before it takes place. This means you can't always purchase tickets early in the game because they (and therefore you) won't know which airport they'll be flying out of.

forms, agendas or other handouts based on your anticipated head count. Make travel arrangements for yourself or your speakers—whoever will be hitting the road on your company's behalf. Send press kits to local and regional newspapers.

Countdown Item 4
One Week Ahead

Contact the hotel's sales or catering people to give them an approximate attendance count and make sure they've got everything squared away. Think of this as being a friendly nag—if they're not sure about any item or if they're not available, keep after them until you know it's done, and done properly.

Countdown Item 5
Two Days Ahead

Call the sales or catering people again and give them your final head count. You can also take this opportunity to check once more that everything's been taken care of and will be ready for you on arrival.

Smart Tip
Remove all ashtrays from the room before your event and post a no-smoking sign or two if there isn't one already posted. Also make sure you post a sign that prohibits cell phone use. Smokers and phone addicts can indulge outside the room during breaks.

▲

The Complete Environment

The secret to a successful program lies in more than intelligently presented subject matter. Audience comfort is a key factor but one that can be easy to forget or ignore. "Our nature as speakers, trainers, and presenters is to assume that our sole responsibility is for our presentation," Larry Smith of National Electrical Seminars in Omaha, Nebraska, cautions. "We're so focused on the presentation that we can easily overlook the complete speaking environment. It's altogether too easy to put the blame for distractions on the meeting planner or elsewhere and press on with our lecture.

"Controlling the complete environment is ultimately our responsibility," Larry adds. "Room temperature, lighting, audio, seating, noisy door latches, extension cord trip hazards—even room cleanliness—reflects directly on us."

Countdown Item 6
The Day Before the Seminar

If you're traveling to an out-of-town site, today's the day you want to arrive. Give yourself plenty of time to recover from jet lag. Familiarize yourself with the layout of the room you'll work in, and where the restrooms, pay phones, copiers, restaurants, lobbies, and other facilities are located. Go over things like meals and snacks with hotel staff. Make sure all site-provided equipment—things like microphones, projectors, video players, and monitors—are present, accounted for, and in good working order. Make sure, too, that you know how to operate them. "When you hear stories about a presenter's multimedia presentation crashing, the cause of the failure is generally lack of familiarity with the equipment and sheer panic," says Larry Smith of National Electrical Seminars in Omaha, Nebraska.

Check seating arrangements and room temperature. "The room is too cold for the audience if we feel cold when wearing a suit coat or sports jacket while speaking," Smith advises. "If we're sweating and the audience is lethargic, it's too warm. If the thermostat has a tamper-resistant cover, you will have to contact maintenance to make the adjustment. Let your audience know you're concerned with their comfort.

"Your presentation and everything associated with it will reflect directly on you," Smith says. "If the temperature in the room is too warm, participants will walk away thinking 'That was a great presentation—I just wish it hadn't been so hot in there.' "

While you're checking on these details, don't forget to examine phone and electrical outlets for your electronic credit card terminal. If something isn't right, complain now instead of having your participants complain tomorrow. If you'll have assistants, go over your battle plan so everyone knows what's expected and how to do it right.

Beware!
The Federal Trade Commission's Mail or Telephone Order Merchandise Rule applies to anybody taking orders placed via fax, e-mail, internet, telephone or mail. (That's you.) Take a look at this rule in "The Ticking Clock" on page 104.

Countdown Item 7
The Big Day

You and any assistants should arrive an hour or even two hours early to check the room setup, temperature, equipment, and noise factors one more time. "External noise of any kind, including noisy door latches, will destroy your audience's concentration," Smith advises. "Some tape over a door latch will silence it."

Also make sure your physical seating plan is exactly what you'd envisioned. For sample seating plans, turn to pages 94 and 95. Set up tables for registration, handouts, and products. Get your credit card terminal up and running. Remove ashtrays and set out no-smoking and no-cell-phone signs. Then greet your participants, get going and have fun!

Registration

OK, you've designed your seminar. You've gone through a seminar countdown. You're doing great! But there's more to the life of a seminar professional. How about getting all those potential attendees from glimmer-of-interest to registered participant? Once your advertising goes out, you're on call. You have to be ready to answer questions and accept registrations. Some of the following tips apply more to public seminars than to private, but even if you're going the private route, read up!

- *Be professional, please.* Make sure your phone is answered by someone who can speak knowledgeably about the seminar, the speakers, and your company. Have your computer up and running and your mailing list or other database program humming so you can take your registrant's information over the phone, including credit card information.

- *Be copasetic and confirm.* Read all the information back to your caller to make sure it's correct. Confirm the name of the seminar, the date, the location, and the time. If you offer more than one seminar, make sure you've got your participant down for the right program in the right city on the right date. You don't want anyone flying to Orlando in October when the seminar is in Memphis in March!

- *Follow up fast.* If potential participants call during off-hours, call them back promptly. Don't lose attendees by failing to act when their enthusiasm is high.

- *Answer your mail.* You may receive up to half your registrations by mail. Make sure you register applicants for the correct event, date, and city and send them a confirmation package—a confirmation letter, ticket and any necessary materials—as soon as possible. You may want to wait two weeks after depositing checks to make sure they've cleared your bank, but don't delay any longer. Again, you want to respond while their enthusiasm is high, and your confirmation package can act as additional promotional material, which is a good thing.

- *Read it right.* If you can't make out somebody's scrawl, call and ask for clarification. (You can do this because you'll have provided a space for a phone number on the registration form.)

Smart Tip Tip...

"Sound reinforcement systems are notoriously temperamental," seminar entrepreneur Larry Smith says. "We've been told to always test the sound system prior to the presentation; that's good advice. There's just one problem. We're testing it in an empty room. When the room is full of people, it may be necessary to make another adjustment. Have the technician standing by."

Hotel Hell

"The single most frustrating task in our business," Larry Smith of Omaha, Nebraska-based National Electrical Seminars advises, "is dealing with hotels. Disaster avoidance dictates arriving a day early to ensure that everything is set up properly. On the day of the presentation, be in the meeting room at least an hour before you expect the first participant to arrive.

"Expect torn and patched projection screens," the certified code trainer says, "malfunctioning audio systems, the wrong table layout, inadequate heating and cooling systems, insufficient electrical outlets, and bad food. Regardless of how bad things may appear, stay cool. Work with whoever is in charge of the setup. Blowing off steam won't adjust a bad PA system; working with the person who knows how to adjust it will."

The Light Fantastic

Among the many mechanical aspects to check and double-check before your presentation is lighting, which can have a bigger effect than you might imagine.

"The best type of lighting we can hope for is incandescent," explains Larry Smith of National Electrical Seminars in Omaha, Nebraska. "It's the ordinary type of lighting we have in our homes—ordinary light bulbs. Incandescent lighting is wonderful because its color temperature is warm (yellow). Under incandescent lighting we look like we've got a great suntan. The colors of visual aids (LCD projected slides, overhead projected slides, etc.) will leap off the screen under incandescent light.

"Daylight is the worst lighting of all," Smith adds. "It's the coldest color temperature. Do everything you can to keep daylight off the projection screen; it will completely wash the color out of your slides.

"Another type of lighting that is harsh is cool white fluorescent," Smith continues. "Its color temperature is very cold. It's commonly used in stores, offices, and classrooms. It kills color. Unfortunately, it's commonly used in meeting rooms, and if a fluorescent light fixture is directly over your projection screen, it's big trouble. Don't hesitate to have bulbs removed from fixtures that are near the screen."

- *Say hey.* On seminar day, set up your registration table at the entrance to your meeting room. Greet your participants warmly. Have copies of the agenda, workbook, and other handouts ready to, well, hand out. You'll also want a list of registered participants so you can cross these people off as they check in.

Walk-Ins

Most seminar professionals garner the majority of their participants through direct mail and word-of-mouth referrals, which means they get more than 90 percent of their registration before the big day. But if you'll do a lot of newspaper and radio advertising, say for a big-name speaker or for a wealth-building seminar that appeals to the masses, then you'll need to be prepared for a lot of walk-ins. Even for a smaller program, you'll probably get a few. Just like down at the beauty shop where a walk-in is somebody who hasn't made an appointment, in the seminar world a walk-in is somebody who hasn't preregistered.

Since your walk-ins will become sit-ins once they've paid their admission, you'll also need to think about seating. Make sure you've got extra chairs—and workspaces if it's a

Smart Tip

Tip...

Being a good presenter is like being a good guest: You do your best when you don't overstay your welcome. "I always try to time it a little bit short," says Shawnee, Kansas, seminar professional Dr. Jerry Old. "I think it's good, when you're really, really getting people's interest, to quit. Don't talk until they're ready for you to quit—always leave them wanting more."

seminar where desk space will be needed—and room to put them so everybody has a view of the podium. If you expect a lot of walk-ins, go for a facility that doesn't have fixed seating so you can adjust as necessary.

Be sure to bring enough materials for those walk-ins, too. You don't want an extra warehouse load—which would be cost-inefficient and also make for extra labor in dragging them around—but you do want to have enough to go around. It also pays to have one set of each workbook and handout ready to photocopy with the bindings and staples removed; make arrangements with the hotel staff to use a copier. If more walk-ins show up than you have materials for, you can run off copies and hand them out, and then send their recipients the "real" bound version by mail along with a coupon for 10 percent off the next seminar.

Seating by the Numbers

If you'll host a big crowd, you'll need to decide on either open or assigned seating. The former is easy—just like down at the local cinema, people sit wherever they find an unoccupied seat that's to their liking. For assigned seating, however, you'll need ushers to guide folks to the appropriate sections. You'll also need some way to determine on the ticket who's sitting where. You might use color-coded tickets, or you might want to arrange seating by the numbers on the tickets—a method that requires you to keep tight control of those tickets and the order in which they're sold.

On Stage!

You've done everything right. You've planned perfectly, promoted to a "T," and gotten everybody registered and seated. Now what? You're on! It's your show. Take it away with your own special magic and these tips:

- *Meet and greet.* Let participants know you're glad they've come. Make them feel welcome. Remember that you want them to enjoy the program so much that they'll report enthusiastically to colleagues, bosses, and friends

Bright Idea

Stick-on name tags are kind of cornball, but they work, especially in interactive formats. Attendees feel like participants instead of mere audience members, everybody gets in a party/intro mood, and you as the presenter can call people by name without having to memorize.

Entertainment Tonight

You don't have to sing and dance to present a viable program, but you do need to amuse and/or enthrall your audience. "The days of classroom style, lecture-based training are over," says Larry Smith of National Electrical Seminars in Omaha, Nebraska. "Today's audiences cannot and will not sit and be lectured to for extended periods of time; they can tolerate lecture-based training for an hour or two at the most. In short order, their attention will wander off into never-never land. They become restless, argumentative, and they learn to dislike training with quiet passion. Audiences desperately want to be entertained; call it entertainment if you like."

Dr. Jerry Old does straightforward talks instead of technical training, but he agrees. "I use a lot of humor and a lot of anecdotes," says the Shawnee, Kansas, seminar provider.

And Nance Cheifetz of Sense of Delight in Novato, California, adds, "We set up our training [sessions] so they're really fun to attend. They're not boring—they're really playful, and people come out with some really good information. It's all interactive."

And it works. "The amount of learning that takes place," Smith concludes, "is proportional to the amount of fun the participants have."

and will be eager to attend your next event. This is a good time to ask people about themselves and sound them out about what they hope to learn. Make mental notes!

- *Be a timekeeper.* Start on time, stay on time for coffee and meal breaks, and end on time. Don't worry about latecomers unless there's some major traffic glitch that makes half your audience late—if you stick to your schedule, your participants will, too. If you start late because of traffic glitches, explain why and offer people who are already on-site some sort of nonscheduled participatory exercise they can do that won't make a hole in your program later.

- *Lay your ground rules.* Introduce yourself. Explain your no-smoking and no-cellphone policies. Put the kibosh on tape-recording the program. Why? First, people fiddling with their pocket recorders, checking to see if the tape's run out or the machine's picking up, distract others, and get distracted themselves. Second, people who record the session on their own aren't likely to purchase your carefully packaged audiotapes.

- *Introduce your program.* People are always more comfortable when they know what to expect. Give them an idea of what they'll learn, why it's important, what's expected of them (participation, interaction, questions for you, quizzes for them, or whatever you've designed), how long each portion of the program will last, times that you plan to break (e.g., 10 A.M. for coffee break, noon for lunch), and what you think they'll achieve.

- *Put on the pizazz!* The best presenters are enthusiastic, high-energy people who are vitally interested in their subjects and their audience and can communicate their thoughts and ideas in an entertaining fashion. You don't have to be Robin Williams, but you don't want to emulate Ed Sullivan, either. Your stellar promotional materials have got your participants in the door—keep up the momentum with a high-caliber presentation.

- *End on a high note.* Send participants home feeling excited and enthusiastic. Just because the day's at an end is no reason to slack off. Remember again that word-of-mouth and repeat customers are your two absolute best sources of advertising.

- *Be your personal best.* Remember to hand out evaluation forms after the program and to encourage people to complete them. Evaluations are invaluable tools for assessing your personal best (and worst) and those of your presenters. Most people want you to succeed, so they'll be happy to give you feedback—just make sure your form isn't so long and complex that it feels like a high school history final. Refresh your memory with another look at the evaluation form on page 35 in Chapter 2. Copy the form and use it for your company or power up your desktop-publishing software and modify our form to suit your needs.

Once you've got those completed forms in hand, don't forget to make use of them. It's extremely important to sit down as soon as possible after your program and go over them—otherwise you forget the specifics of that particular seminar and the evaluations lose their relevance.

Which Days Are Better for Seminars?

Day	Pros	Cons
Sunday	Good for personal development seminars like financial planning or successful dressing	Not so hot for business-related programs because people don't like to spend their off-time on office stuff
Monday	Good if you use it to kick off a five-day business program	Everybody suffers the Monday blues and crankies, trying desperately to regroup after a weekend of downtime, so this is not a good day for starting a one- or two-day program.
Tuesday	Good for business seminars or for programs aimed at seniors or stay-at-home parents	
Wednesday	Good for business seminars or for programs aimed at seniors or stay-at-home parents	
Thursday	Good! If your program ends today, participants who've come from out-of-town can schedule a three-day weekend.	
Friday	If you've got a one-day program, business attendees may perceive your seminar as a sort of bonus, the beginning of a three-day weekend.	
Saturday	Good for personal programs like confidence- and wealth-building or gardening	

Hotel Confirmation Letter

June 5, 200x

Ms. Jennifer Turnez, Meeting Sales Manager
Oakmont Hotel & Conference Center
3 Oakmont Center
Oakmont, CA 90000

Dear Ms. Turner:

I enjoyed speaking with you yesterday regarding our upcoming TravelTeach seminar and look forward to working with you. This letter will serve to confirm the arrangements we agreed upon:

Seminar Dates: October 6 and 7, 200x

Seminar Times: 9 A.M. to 4 P.M., October 6 and 9 A.M. to 3 P.M., October 7

Our program should be listed as "Thinking European for Business Travelers."

Please set up the room for 20 participants in accordance with the enclosed diagram. We will expect a block of 22 double-occupancy guest rooms from October 5 through October 8.

Our food and beverage requirements are as follows:

10/6: Coffee and croissants for 20 at 8:30 A.M.
 Coffee, tea, and scones for 20 at 11 A.M.
 Coffee and crepes for 20 at 2 P.M.
 Water in room throughout seminar, refreshed with each food/beverage service
 Dinner of chicken Kiev, rice, mixed greens, coffee or tea, and trifle in the Oak BayRoom for 35 at 6 P.M.

1 Eiffel Court, Paris, TX 75000   (000) 000-4500   TravelTeach@hotl.com

10/7: Coffee and croissants for 20 at 8:30 A.M.
Coffee, tea, and scones for 20 at 11 A.M.
Coffee and crepes for 20 at 2 P.M.
Water in room throughout seminar, refreshed with each food/beverage service

We will require one each of the following equipment items:
Microphone
Video player
Slide projector
Video monitor
Screen

Per our agreement, our rates will be as follows:

Meeting room	$ 175
Food and beverage service	150
Dinner	200
Meeting equipment	340
Guest rooms (22)	1,980
Total	$2,845

We'll expect a contract on the above arrangements within the next week. Don't hesitate to call with any questions.

Very best,

Jillian Jordan

Jillian Jordan
TravelTeach Seminars

JJ/aa

1 Eiffel Court, Paris, TX 75000   (000) 000-4500   TravelTeach@hotl.com

Meeting Planner Form

Seminar: _____

Meeting location: _____ Telephone: _____

Address: _____

City, state, zip: _____

Date(s): _____

Day(s): _____

Estimated count: _____

Room Name: _____ Room capacity: _____

1st day rm. rental: _____ 2nd day rm. rental: _____

Menu 1st day: _____

_____

_____

Menu 2nd day: _____

_____

_____

Coffee: _____

Gratuity: _____ Sales tax: _____

Sleeping room rate: _____ Reservation no. _____

Ground Floor: ❑ Yes ❑ No ❑ Nonsmoking ❑ Smoking

Days reserved: _____

Commercial room rate: _____

Sales & catering contact: _____

Today's date: _____

Projection Screens

The tried-and-true motion picture standard for projection screens is:

1. The row most distant from the screen should be no more than six times the width of the screen from the screen.

2. The row closest to the screen should be no closer than two times the width of the screen to the screen.

3. The width of the rows should not exceed six times the width of the screen.

4. The bottom of the screen should be at least 36 inches above the floor.

I call it the six-two-six rule. It's no good to create an attention-grabbing visual presentation if everyone in your audience isn't able to see it. How often have you seen a presenter throw an overhead slide on a projector and then say to the audience, "I know this is too small for you to see, but..." The visual part of the message is nonexistent and becomes a distraction for the audience.

The screen has to be sized to fit the audience. As the presenter, it's ultimately your responsibility, and you can't rely on anyone else to do it correctly.

Screen Width	Last Row No Further Than _____ to the Screen	First Row No Closer Than _____ to the Screen
4 feet	24 feet	8 feet
5 feet	30 feet	10 feet
6 feet	36 feet	12 feet
8 feet	48 feet	16 feet
10 feet	60 feet	20 feet
12 feet	72 feet	24 feet

Notes:

Classroom-Style Seating Plan

Slide Projector & Screen		Podium		Video Monitor & Player

Desk/Chair Desk/Chair Desk/Chair Desk/Chair

Desk/Chair Desk/Chair Desk/Chair Desk/Chair

Desk/Chair Desk/Chair Desk/Chair Desk/Chair

Desk/Chair Desk/Chair Desk/Chair Desk/Chair

Desk/Chair Desk/Chair Desk/Chair Desk/Chair

Chair Chair

Refreshment Table

Registration/Products Table

Entrance

Seating for Success

Style	Description	Pros	Cons
Classroom	Picture your third grade classroom: rows of desk-size tables with aisles in between and the teacher (that's you) facing them from a center podium	Good for lecture formats where your participants will take a lot of notes; can accommodate a large number of people	Not conducive to interaction/participation formats because it's hard for people to see people behind them
Conference Room	Board-of-directors version: a long table with participants seated along both sides and at one end; the presenter presides at the head of the table. Or go for the knights-of-the-round-table version: the same thing but with a round instead of oblong table.	Good for interaction/participation programs and for note-taking	Cannot accommodate many people unless the table stretches so long that people have to holler down its length (defeating the purpose of interaction)
Banquet Room	Wedding or retirement dinner version: round tables that seat four to six each, staggered around the presenter, who faces them at the front of the room	Good for networking and keynote speech during meal formats	Can be noisy and distracting, and hard on whoever has to sit with his back to the presenter (or rather try to face his dinner and the speaker at the same time without contortions or spills)
Theater	Church or country auction version: row upon row of chairs lined up with the presenter presiding from the podium at the front	Accommodates large groups well	Not conducive to interaction/participation formats and bad for short folks who can't see over the heads in front of them

Seminar Presenter's Bag of Tricks

Like the wily cartoon character Felix the Cat, the savvy seminar presenter brings a bag of tricks along that contains everything he or she could possibly need to get and keep the program going. What's in this magic bag (or box or briefcase)? Take a peek; then make copies to use for your own company, or modify this list to suit your needs.

❑ Copies of all contracts and arrangements with hotel or conference center

❑ Cheat sheet listing registered participants and where they're from (e.g., which company or association chapter)

❑ Registration forms

❑ Name tags

❑ Credit card terminal

❑ Cash receipt book

❑ Change box for making back-of-the-room product sales

❑ All equipment not supplied by the site

   ___Overhead projector and transparencies

   ___Video player and videos to use during session

   ___Microphone

   ___Laser pointer

   ___Dry erase marker board and markers

   ___Tape deck and tapes to use during session

❑ Program notes and highlights for presenter, including intros of any additional speakers

❑ Workbooks and other handout materials

❑ Sales materials for upcoming seminars

❑ Evaluation forms

❑ On-the-spot stationery supplies: scissors, masking tape, cellophane tape, push pins, pens, pencils, paper tablets, stapler, and staples (for making and posting last-minute directional signs, notes, writing receipts, name tags, etc.)

❑ Back-of-the-room products:

   ___Audiotapes

   ___Videotapes

   ___Books

   ___Other: _____

From Back Door to Back of the Room
Inventory and Shipping

As a savvy seminar professional, you don't have to worry about inventory the way a retailer or restaurateur does—you don't need to keep a dozen size 12 dresses on the racks in your store or figure out how many chicken legs you'll need for your diner for the week. But you do need a supply of your stock in trade: your workbooks, evaluation sheets, and any

back-of-the-room products. And, as we've said before, you'll need to be prepared to send a certain number of products to folks who order on your web site or call to request tapes (or whatever) for their boss, sister, or mum. In this chapter, we explore the ins and outs of inventory—the stuff you've got on your garage or office shelves—and discover the secrets to successful packing and shipping.

Inventory

Inventory refers to the materials you need to have on hand, like tickets and workbooks, as well as the products you sell. And as we've said, you lucky seminar professional, you don't need a lot!

Take a Ticket

If you'll host large-audience public seminars, you'll want tickets, which we've touched on in our start-up costs chapter. A wise way to go is to print universal tickets, which doesn't mean that you can use them anywhere in the universe, but that they aren't imprinted with a specific date. This way you can use the same run for a seminar you give in October as for one you give in May. You save money by having them printed in bulk, and you can use the same tickets until they run out.

Print the tickets with the name of your company and any ground rules you'd like to lay

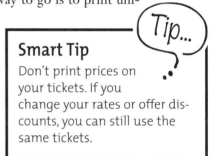

Smart Tip

Don't print prices on your tickets. If you change your rates or offer discounts, you can still use the same tickets.

about smoking or tape-recording. Make sure the tickets aren't a cinch to copy—instead of cookie-cutting them out of copy paper, number them or print them on colored or heavy stock. Take a peek at the sample ticket below for an example of a universal ticket.

Universal Ticket

No.238

Event:
Date:

Please note that audio and videotape recording are prohibited.

TravelTeach Seminars

Teaching the World to Travel Smart

Smoking is permitted only in designated areas.

Admits One
No.238

Evaluation Evolution

The trusty evaluation form, as we've explained, also counts as part of your inventory. Like your tickets, you may want to keep it as nonspecific as possible so you can use the same one over and over. Or since it's a simple one-page form that can be inexpensively photocopied, let it evolve along with your company. If you find as you go along that you are using other presenters besides yourself, let your form encompass questions about them, too, as well as about the quality or desirability of meals and snacks or about your ticket-sales approach.

Copy the evaluation form starting on page 35 to use for your company, or fire up your desktop-publishing program and modify it to suit your own needs.

The Product Scene

You know one big reason for spending the time, effort, and yes, money, to develop back-of-the-room products: to earn extra income from your seminars. The ability to make 30 to 60 percent of your income from these sales is a pretty powerful motivator. But there is another important reason for developing products: When people attend your programs, they feel empowered, excited and ready to take on the world. Having something tangible to take away with them promotes retention, allows them to revisit

Work Smart

Providing workbooks helps your participants feel that they've gotten their money's worth—besides the brain food you've provided, they've got something tangible they can hold in their hands and take home with them to refer to later, show to friends and colleagues, or paste in their scrapbooks. A workbook can be a fairly involved book that offers various exercises, insights, and information. But you might also consider offering a concise pamphlet that emphasizes the main points of a talk but doesn't contain any work sheets. Take a look at the sample workbook cover on page 100.

If you hire presenters, they provide the material but leave it to you to make copies for participants. Remember that while your goal is to project a professional image, you don't need to spend a fortune on workbooks. You can have them professionally printed or copied, but don't worry about perfect binding or four-color graphics.

Smart Stuff

S E M I N A R S

Presents

Gilding the Gift Basket

Super Sales for Gift Basket Retailers

by
Malcolm Johonsson

Smart Stuff Seminars

87 Lingon Lane
Havenleaf, FL 30000
123.125.2356

For information about this seminar or any of our other stellar programs,
please call or write, or visit our web site at
www.smartstuffseminars.com.

the information and the empowerment again and again, and keeps you in the "New! Now!" section of their memory banks so they'll be eager to attend your next program.

As a newbie, you probably won't make a tremendous amount on product sales—it takes time to build up a reputation and a following. But it's definitely worth working toward. What if you're hiring out speakers and don't star in the seminars yourself? You can still earn income from product sales by selling your speakers' merchandise on consignment.

You'll need to have a contract or agreement with your speakers covering all the details of product sales: which products to sell, how many of each item to offer, how much to charge for each, and how to handle any unsold items. You'll also need to spell out how you'll split the profits—usually speakers and promoters each take a 50 percent share, but this can range from 20 to 60 percent, depending on how you want to work it. Be sure to specify whether the profits you're sharing are net or gross.

Shooting Schedule

DVDs and videotapes are an intrinsic part of the seminar industry. Demo videos serve as "auditions" to help speakers bureaus and potential clients determine what your skills are. Some presenters use other speakers' videos in their seminars to help illustrate a particular point or segment. And of course, videos work as terrific products.

You can make like a Hollywood hotshot and have your video taped at the videographer's studio ("Hold all phone calls, dahling; we're shooting"), or you can have the videographer film you at a live seminar. Keep in mind that a professional-quality film needs a pro video cameraperson and the proper lighting. Even though today's camcorders are pretty slick, a film shot by your brother-in-law the accountant is going to look—and feel—like a home movie shot by an amateur. Plus, by going the amateur route you can run into duping problems that you won't have when you go with a pro who can provide this service at better quality and a lower price than you'd get on your own.

Bright Idea

Approach your local radio station. They've got the equipment and the expertise, and they'll often do an audiotape for you for far less money than an outsourced studio would charge.

If you're acting as a promoter rather than a speaker, you'll need to have an agreement with your talent to tape and then sell his or her seminar. You'll also need, as we've said earlier, an agreement on sales and the distribution of revenues. Video production can get pricey because you have to add the costs of duping, packaging,

Sign Language

Although you won't need a huge supply, you will need signs— for registration, products, workbooks, and autograph tables, if you'll use them. (If you're working a small seminar with fewer than 20 participants, for instance, you might want to set participants' handouts on their desks, just like in grade school.)

If your speakers are big names, or are on their way to big-namedom (e.g., authors at a sci-fi convention or romance novel conference), an autograph table can boost product sales. After all, if a participant is motivated to buy a book after sitting in on a seminar by its author, she'll be even more motivated if she has an autographed copy.

Keep your signs simple. "Registration," "Please Take One" for workbooks, "Help Yourself" for freebies from sponsors, and "Autographs" should be all you need to say. Gather up your signs after each seminar so you can reuse them, and store them with enough care to keep them looking good.

and storing the tapes onto the initial production fees. (For more information, see page 55 in Chapter 4.)

The same tenets hold for audio CD production and sales. They can be a big asset, but they must be professionally produced. You sitting at your kitchen table reading a script into your boom box is going to sound like you sitting at your kitchen table, except tinny and muddy as well. Make sure you go for the real thing.

Hooked on Books

Books can be a big part of your product scene. You might think seminar stars pen their volumes and become bestselling authors before hitting the lecture circuit. Not. At least not always. Gail Hahn of Fun*cilitators in Reston, Virginia, for example, developed her book as a part of her start-up plan. "I decided I needed a book fast to earn credibility," she says, "to have a 'brochure' that people didn't throw away, to say that I am an author and therefore an expert on the topic. I didn't want to waste time and effort

Bright Idea

Check with your community college. They may have a video department that can provide professional services in exchange for student credits on your film and a professional reference from your company to use on their resumes. Or go with a local cable TV station—like your local radio station, they've got the equipment and expertise and will often provide it at far less expense than an outsourced firm.

seeking a publisher, and didn't want to wait a year or more to get it accepted and published. I wrote the book and had it on the streets in ten weeks. The actual printing took about three weeks."

Let's Shop!

What should you offer as back-of-the-room products besides books, CDs, and videos? It all depends on the ambience you're aiming for. Besides looking at what other seminar professionals are selling, pore over mail order catalogs and take a spin through gift shops down at the mall. If you're doing motivational seminars, for instance, look for items like coffee mugs, pens, small prints or posters, refrigerator magnets, or desktop goodies that bear inspirational sayings. Can you do something similar?

If you see something you like and you think it might translate into your own products, contact vendors and suppliers. You can find them under "Advertising Specialties" in your local Yellow Pages, or check out the various vendors at gift shows held regionally around the country. (Your local or regional chamber of commerce, convention center, or visitors bureau can tell you when one will be in town.)

As a final note, the idea here is not to spend a fortune on products—your main product is the message you're delivering in your seminars, not boutique items. If you don't feel that products are right for your company, don't provide them. And if you feel that you'd rather get into products after you've got a year or so and a bit of capital under your belt, that's fine too.

> ### Bright Idea
> Newsletters make a terrific product. People who are jazzed after your energizing seminar can sign up for quarterly newsletters from you, which can act not only as tip, technique, and news sheets but also as ongoing advertising and promotion for your future programs.

The Shipping Skinny

> ### Smart Tip
> **Tip...**
> To really push the envelope—or package—and for indepth information on mail order tips and techniques, bone up with Entrepreneur's *Start Your Own Mail-Order Business*.

You won't need to spend a lot of time worrying about shipping your products—most of them will be sold at the back of the room. But you'll want to be prepared for those instances where people ask for products to be sent later. And this puts you with one foot over the line into mail order territory.

The important thing to keep in mind here is fulfillment, getting that ordered package from your garage, office, or warehouse to your

Package Pointers

How exactly will you get those packages to your customers? You've seen the TV commercials. Your main choices are UPS, the U.S. Postal Service, and FedEx. Most mail order entrepreneurs use UPS for packages because it's generally cheaper than FedEx, faster than the post office, and also has better tracking capabilities than the post office for items that get lost in the shuffle. If a customer absolutely, positively has to have something overnight, go with FedEx, which has a terrific record for on-time deliveries. Be sure to add shipping charges and any taxes onto your customer's order—this is customary mail order practice.

customer's door. Failure to provide prompt fulfillment will result in more complaints, cancellations, and general compounded daily-type crankiness than just about anything else.

The Ticking Clock

Since you're now treading in mail order territory, you should familiarize yourself with the Federal Trade Commission's Mail or Telephone Order Merchandise Rule, which regulates direct-marketing businesses (that's you with your products!). When the law first went into effect in 1975 it was called the Mail Order Rule—its title has changed to include the word "telephone," but it also applies to orders placed via e-mail, internet, and fax. The Mail or Telephone Order Merchandise Rule applies to almost everything ordered through direct marketing sources. The exceptions are: magazine subscriptions and similar serial deliveries (after the first issue), cash-on-delivery orders, and seeds and growing plants.

The basic premise of the rule is that you must ship a customer's order within the time period specified in your ad or, if you make no time statement, within 30 days of the date you receive a completed order. If you later learn that you cannot ship within those 30 days, you must give your customer either a revised ship date or a statement that you don't have a new date and the reason for the situation. You must also give your customer:

- the choice, if you provide a revised ship date, of accepting the delay or getting a prompt refund of her money
- the choice, if you cannot provide a revised ship date, of accepting the delay or getting a prompt refund of her money as well as reassurance that she can cancel the order and get a refund at any time until you do ship

- a means for your customer to cancel at your expense such as by toll-free telephone or by postage-paid mail

There are various permutations of the above based on various ordering, payment, and shipping scenarios, and you can find yourself flailing in rough seas if you ignore the rule's guidelines, but not to panic! The Federal Trade Commission (FTC) provides a complete guide—everything you ever wanted to know about the rule and then some—on its web site at www.ftc.gov. You can also call the FTC toll-free at (877) FTC-HELP or write to Federal Trade Commission, Consumer Response Center, 600 Pennsylvania Ave. NW, Washington, DC 20580.

7

The Projection Room
Your Business Equipment

Although you may spend a fair amount of time traveling the country with your seminars, you'll need an office. This will be your command center, the heart of your business, so stocking it with the proper equipment is vital to your success. You'll need some of the things that every business office needs, like a computer and a telephone. Others, like an overhead projector, are specialized. And, again—you lucky seminar professional, you—some of these things are often provided by hotels and meeting centers, which means that you don't need to purchase them yourself.

We've provided a handy checklist (see page 121) to help you determine what you will need, what you already have on hand, and which items can be rented from the meeting facility. Die-hard shoppers may want to rush out and buy every item brand-spanking new, but don't be too quick a draw with the old credit card, at least not until you've finished this chapter.

After you've read it through, run down the checklist and evaluate your stock. Is your computer seminar production-ready, or is it an antique that won't be able to keep up the pace? Does your answering machine receive audible messages, or does it tend to garble crucial information? How about that printer? Can it produce professional-looking materials in short order, or does it take ages to spit out a solitary quivery page?

Now, checklist in hand, let's take a whirlwind virtual shopping spree. Ready, steady, go!

Wait a second. Let's discuss something first. There's always the buy of a lifetime and there's always the ultimate fancy-shmancy tiptop of the line. What we're looking for here are the low-end and middle-of-the-road models. You can trade up to the Rolls Royce of computers and other equipment after your business is up and running and able to pay for its upgrades.

Office Equipment

First up, let's take a look at your office equipment, the tools of the trade that will get your operation up and running and keep it going efficiently.

Computer Glitterati

Your computer will be the luminary of your office setup, coordinating your invoicing, accounting, word-processing, database, and desktop-publishing activities—not to mention co-starring in all web site activities and e-mail correspondence. It may be your most important start-up purchase. If you already own a computer, you'll want to make sure it's capable of handling the tasks you'll assign it.

Your new computer should house a 2.4 GHz Intel Pentium 4 (or its equivalent, the Athlon XP 2100+) with a Windows XP operating system

Smart Tip

Want to keep equipment costs way down? Consider launching from a business incubator, where services and equipment are shared among several businesses.

since this is what all but clunker found-at-garage-sale software packages are geared for. To run your software properly, you will need at least 512MB RAM, plus a hard drive with at least 80GB of storage, a rewritable DVD drive (or at least a rewritable CD-ROM drive), and also a 56Kbps modem. You can expect to pay from $1,000 to $1,500 for a good name-brand desktop computer, with prices increasing as you add on goodies.

If you'll travel—and especially if you'll be doing multimedia presentations—you'll need a laptop computer as well. A well-appointed model—with at least 256MB RAM and a 20GB hard drive—will run about $800 to $1,000.

Shot through Gauze

If you plan to produce your own web site or your own advertising materials (or both), you'll definitely want a digital camera. With one of these wondrous tools, you simply snap a photo of your product, hook the camera up to your computer, move your mouse around a bit—and presto!—you've got the picture of your product right in your desktop-publishing program. Expect to pay from $130 to $350 for a good-quality digital camera. (Look for one with at least 3 megapixels of resolution for super-clear images that will translate well into your brochures and other print materials.)

Once the photo is in your computer, you can manipulate it in all sorts of interesting ways, acting as your own photofinishing expert. You can crop it, expand it, zoom in or out on various features, blur the edges for that shot-through-gauze look (helpful if you're taking a picture of yourself with wrinkles or zits), make it look like a watercolor, pastel, or oil painting, ad infinitum. This stuff is not only great for business purposes, it's a heck of a lot of fun! Some digital cameras, like Kodak's, come complete with the software you need to manipulate photos. Or you can purchase any

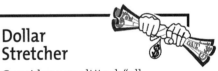

▲

number of programs, from Adobe's Photoshop Elements, priced at about $100, to Adobe's full-bore, technically brilliant (and extremely user hostile) Photoshop, which costs about $600.

You may also want to consider a scanner, a nifty gadget that imports or "pastes" graphics from just about any printed medium—books, photographs, original art, or postcards, for example—into your desktop-publishing program.

Purring Printers

A good printer is a must. You'll want to produce all sorts of promotional materials, invoices, receipts, packing slips, mailing labels, thank-you notes, contracts, statements, and sundry other materials, and they all need to look polished and professional. The materials you produce will be a direct reflection of your company. Shaky, faint dot-matrix printing looks amateurish. Sharp, bold graphics and print give your business an aura of confidence and success.

Beware!

Remember that you can't use anything on your web site that somebody else holds a copyright on, including graphics, artwork, and text. Make sure the material you scan into your own work is copyright-free, or in the case of hired-on speakers, that you have permission to use the material before you import it.

Read All About It!

The written word is a powerful learning tool. One of your first steps in your new venture should be to read everything you can, not just about the specifics of seminar production but about starting a small business and about marketing and sales techniques. Blitz the bookstore. Make an assault on your public library.

Your own business library should contain a plethora of reference manuals. For starters, check out the following:

- ❍ *How to Make it Big in the Seminar Business,* by Paul Karasik (McGraw-Hill).
- ❍ *Money Talks: How to Make a Million as a Speaker,* by Alan Weiss (McGraw-Hill).
- ❍ *Become a Recognized Authority In Your Field In 60 Days or Less!* by Robert W. Bly (Alpha).

Don't stop with these. Immerse yourself in your subject. The more you know, the better seminar professional you'll be. Read all about it!

Fortunately, really hot-stuff printers are much less expensive now than ever before. You can purchase a laser or an inkjet, both of which can produce all the wonderful colors of commercial artwork. Color-capable models print more slowly than their black-and-white colleagues, but if you'll be doing lots of marketing materials like brochures and newsletters, then color should be a consideration. You can expect to pay from $100 to $1,000 for a color inkjet or laser printer.

Just the Fax

The fax machine is a must for anybody in business these days. Along with e-mail, it's the method of choice for communicating quickly and clearly with clients and meeting-site personnel. Many customers like to fax information back and forth, and as a savvy marketer, you want to oblige. After all, the easier you make communications, the easier it will be for people to book you. And don't forget faxing lunch orders to that deli down the street! Plan to spend $100 to $350 for a good model.

Smart Tip

Tip...

Because PowerPoint software is used universally for multimedia presentations, it can look universally dull. "The magic is to make PowerPoint not look like PowerPoint," advises Larry Smith of National Electrical Seminars in Omaha, Nebraska. "My clients pay me to be original and creative; I'm not paid to be a clone of someone else. Avoiding the use of PowerPoint templates is one way to stay original—create your own."

Soft on Software

A dazzling array of software lines the shelves of most office supply stores, ready to help you perform every business task—design and print your own checks, develop professional-quality marketing materials, make mailing lists and labels, even act as your own attorney and accountant.

For starters, you'll need a word-processing program, with which you can write correspondence, contracts, sales reports, and whatever else strikes your needs and your fancy. A good basic program such as Microsoft Word or Corel WordPerfect can be had for $60 to $200.

You'll also want an accounting program such as Quicken or Microsoft Money to track your business finances. These are a sort of checkbook on a CD and make record-keeping a breeze. You assign categories such as office supplies and business travel to the checks you write, and at tax time you print out a report showing how much you spent for what. Your accountant not only thanks you but gives you a discount for not having to wade through all your receipts. You can expect to pay $60 to $250 for your cyber-space checkbook.

For those polished marketing materials, you'll want a desktop-publishing program, such as Broderbund's The Print Shop Pro Publisher or Microsoft Publisher. They're user-friendly, with a lot of depth and a lot of breadth, multiple formats, and multiple layouts. And they're customizable. You can expect to pay from $60 to $250.

While you're flexing those graphics-design muscles, you should also consider a presentations software package like Microsoft Power-Point or Corel Presentations. With this type of program, you can make slide shows that incorporate graphs, charts, text, and even animation—your own (more interesting!) version of all those coma-inducing educational films you remember from school. This will be about $200.

Beware!
Like preschoolers, computers are prone to every virus that's making the rounds. As a professional, you can't afford to lose data and time—or to compromise your security—to one of these nasty bugs. Purchase security software that includes an update service, and then use it. Doing so takes about a minute—a nanosecond compared to the time it takes to recover from an attack.

If you plan to build your own web site, you'll want design software like Microsoft's FrontPage, which costs about $169.

Then there's contact management software, which combines an onscreen calendar, date book, address book, and contact-tracking database—a sort of secretary-on-CD. Look for programs like Outlook from Microsoft, ACT from Interact or GoldMine from FrontRange Solutions at prices ranging from $100 to $300.

Beware!
Don't "enhance" your voice mail or answering machine message with background music or a cutesy script. It's not businesslike. Keep it simple. Give your business name—spoken clearly and carefully—and ask callers to leave a short message and a phone number. Thank them for calling and assure them that someone from your office will return their call as soon as possible.

Alternatively, you can purchase an office productivity suite that bundles a bevy of common applications from word processing, presentations, and spreadsheets to contact management and desktop publishing (and in the case of Microsoft, the ubiquitous FrontPage). Priced at $250 to $550, these suites are less expensive than each program purchased individually but don't allow tailoring to your particular wants or needs. The big names here are Microsoft Office, Lotus SmartSuite and Corel WordPerfect Suite.

If you plan to sell a slew of back-of-the-room products on your web site or through direct mail, you may want to purchase mail-order software that tracks customers, orders, and products, and generates reports and even mailing labels. Check out CMS Solo from NewHaven

All the Answers

If you choose not to go with voice mail from your local phone company or a phone system with an integrated answering machine, you'll need to purchase a stand-alone answering machine. (Unless you want to put your business greeting on your home machine and take the risk that your kids might erase your messages, you should purchase a separate machine for your office.)

There are also all sorts of fancy gizmos complete with caller ID, multiple mailboxes, multiple outgoing announcements, and time and date stamps (which simply means they announce the time and date the message was left). Expect to pay $15 to $65.

Software and Mailware Home Office from Core Technologies; expect to pay from $300 to $2,000.

And last but definitely not least, you'll need security software to guard all these goodies from viruses and hackers. Check out products from Symantec, McAfee, and Zone Alarm that incorporate both antivirus and firewall protection; prices range from $50 to $120.

Take a Message

If you start off solo, a substitute you to answer the phone is a necessity—you won't be at your desk every minute or even every day. Even if you send presenters out to do seminars while you stay home to staff the office, you'll sometimes be at the post office or UPS outpost, attending trade shows or interfacing with vendors and suppliers. If you hire a full-time secretary or receptionist, you'll still need a mechanical somebody to answer your office phone when he or she is off duty. A Murphy's Law of business life is that people most often call when: a) you're not in your office; b) you're sitting down to a meal; or c) you're in the bathroom. Another business life law is that an unanswered phone is extremely unprofessional.

So you'll need to think about who—or what—will act as your secretary when you're not available. One solution is voice mail, the phone company's answer to the answering machine, with a few nice twists.

Like an answering machine, voice mail takes your messages when you're not in the office. If you have call waiting, a feature that discreetly

Smart Tip

As a rule of thumb, you should have one outside telephone line for every five employees, depending on call volume.

beeps to announce an incoming call while you're already on the phone, and you choose not to answer that second call, voice mail will take a message for you. With voice mail, as with many answering machines, you can access your messages from a remote location.

Voice mail costs depend on your local phone company and the features you choose, but you can expect to pay in the range of $6 to $20 a month.

Hello Central

Now for the telephone itself. You'll want one line for handling phone calls and another for your fax machine and ISP, unless you plan to transmit information and conduct all your research late at night or in the wee hours of the morning. Computers and fax machines use phones the way teenagers do—when they're transmitting, no one else can possibly get through. So unless you want to risk having callers receive a seemingly endless busy signal or empty ring—which is fatal for a business—you'll need to have a separate line.

With three lines coming into your home, two will be for your office. Therefore, you'll want a two-line phone so you can put one on hold while you're answering the other. You can divide up the three lines any way you like: You might put your home line and your business line on the two-line phone, leaving the third line for your fax machine and modem.

Or you might put the business and fax-modem line on the two-line phone, leaving your home line in the kitchen or den. The idea behind either of these choices is that you can call out on your home or fax-modem line (when it's not in use) and leave the business line for incoming calls.

Whichever option you choose, you'll want the telephone itself to have two lines that can be put on hold. This way, business callers can't hear you explaining to your children why they can't have a nose ring when they call you collect from the mall.

A speaker is also a nice feature, especially for all those on-hold-forever calls to your banker, attorney, insurance company, or whoever. Your hands are free to work on financial data or your latest advertising materials, your shoulder remains un-hunched, and there's no earring jabbing you in the back of the head while you listen to Muzak and wait your turn.

You can expect to pay about $40 to $150 for a two-line speakerphone with caller ID, call waiting, auto redial, memory dial, digital answering machine, flashing lights, mute button, and other assorted goodies.

Smart Tip

Tip...

Don't pay extra for equipment. Negotiate! If you are polite but firm, you can sometimes get the hotel to discount or even throw in use of audiovisual equipment along with the price of the meeting room.

Lightning Strikes Again

A surge protector safeguards your electronic equipment from power spikes during storms or outages. Your battery backup will double as a surge protector for your computer hard drive, or CPU, and monitor, but you'll want protection for those other valuable office allies, your printer, fax machine, and copier. They don't need a battery backup because no data will be lost if the power goes out, and a surge protector will do the job for a lot less money. If you've got a fax machine, be sure the surge protector also defends its phone line. You can expect to pay in the range of $15 to $50 for a surge protector.

> ## Smart Tip
> Tip...
>
> Never send a piece of paper out of your office unless you've kept a copy. You can always print two copies of every document you generate on your computer, keeping one as a file copy.

Cool and Calculating

What do calculators and telephones have in common? A numbered keypad and an important place on your desk. Even though your computer probably has an on-board calculator program, it helps to have the real thing close at hand. You can do quick calculations without zipping around through cyberspace, and with the paper tape, you can check your work. Expect to pay $5 to $20 for a battery-operated model and up to $50 for a plug-in job.

Laugh at Lightning

You should invest in a UPS, or uninterruptible power supply (not to be confused with UPS, the package service), for your computer system, especially if you live in an area where lightning or power surges are frequent occurrences. If you're a computer newbie, you may not realize that even a flicker of power loss can shut down your computer, causing it to forget all the data you've carefully entered during your current work session, or—the ultimate horror—fry your computer's brains entirely. With a UPS in your arsenal, you won't lose power to your system when the power fails or flickers. Instead, the unit flashes red and sounds a warning, giving you ample time to shut down your computer.

If you'll be spending a lot of time on the internet, which accesses the World Wide Web through the telephone, you want to be sure that your UPS includes phone line protection. You can expect to pay $60 to $200 and up for one of these power pals.

Paper Cloning

The copier is an optional item, but as you grow you may find it a necessary luxury for running off workbooks, evaluation sheets, and other handouts. It's far easier to run off one copy or 50 in your own office than to have to run down to the copy center every time the need arises. Good, business-quality desktop copiers range from $100 to $500.

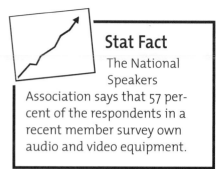

Stat Fact

The National Speakers Association says that 57 percent of the respondents in a recent member survey own audio and video equipment.

Bound for Glory

If you've purchased a copier, you may also want to invest in a spiral binding machine. With one of these low-tech gizmos, you can bind workbooks and other materials with plastic bindings and clear plastic, simulated leather, or vinyl covers. Expect to pay $400 to $2,000 for a binding machine, $15 to $60 per 100 covers, and $12 to $25 per 100 binding spines.

Take a Seat

Office furniture is another optional item. It's important that your work environment is comfortable and ergonomic, but if you're homebased it's perfectly acceptable to start off with an old door set on cinder blocks for a desk and an egg crate for your files. When you're ready to go the big step toward real office furniture for that oh-so-professional look, you've got a stunning array of possibilities to choose from.

We shopped the big office supply warehouse stores and found midrange desks from $200 to $300, a computer work center for under $200, printer stands from $50 to $75, two-drawer letter-size file cabinets (which can double as your printer stand) from $40 to $100, and a four-shelf bookcase for $70.

Chairs are a very personal matter. Some people like the dainty secretary's chair for its economy of space; others want the tonier high-back executive model. There are chairs with pneumatic height adjustments, chairs that automatically adjust to your spine position throughout the day, and chairs that massage your body while you exercise your brain. Prices range from $50 to $200, depending on how elegant and/or ergonomic you choose to go.

Seminar Equipment

OK, you know what you'll need as far as office tools. Now let's look at what you might want to purchase in the way of special equipment for your programs. Keep in mind that hotels, conference centers, and other meeting facilities will generally provide these items for you, which saves not only on money but on the schlep factor. (Dragging TV monitors, projectors, videotape players, and other assorted paraphernalia through a crowded airport may be good exercise, but it's not fun. Having to pass all this stuff through airport security is also not fun.) If the hotel doesn't stock these items, it can probably locate and provide them for you—for a fee, of course. Or you can rent them through a rental center.

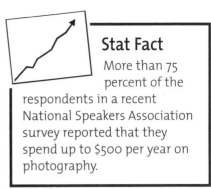

Stat Fact
More than 75 percent of the respondents in a recent National Speakers Association survey reported that they spend up to $500 per year on photography.

We mention them here for two reasons:

1. To give you an idea of what sorts of tools and equipment are out there to be used if you choose
2. So you can purchase or rent them if you plan on operating out of a low-cost facility like a community park hall or church basement that doesn't provide them or if you plan, at some point, to set up your own facility

Hotels and other meeting sites (including community centers and churches) generally provide podiums, tables, and chairs at no extra charge, but be sure to check on what exactly is included. Don't take anything for granted.

Equipment Expenses

To give you an idea how much you can expect to budget, check out the costs of software, equipment, and supplies for two hypothetical seminar companies, TravelTeach Seminars and So Romantic Seminars starting on page 123. TravelTeach, a homebased newbie with no employees except its owner, so far has a net profit of $20,000. The fledgling business counts as its equipment resources an inexpensive computer system and an LED printer, and rents any necessary equipment from the meeting site.

So Romantic, up and running for three years, makes its base in an industrial park office near the airport, employs a secretary and an assistant in addition to the owner, and tabulates annual net profits of $200,000. So Romantic boasts a top-of-the-line computer system for its owner, inexpensive computers for its employees, a laser printer, a combo fax machine/scanner, a copier, and various publishing and marketing software programs that have caught its owner's eye over the years.

You've Got It!

The buzzword in the biz these days is "multimedia." And why not? With all the state-of-the-art audio, video, and computer technology out there, it's exciting to consider the possibilities. Multiple screens, multiple images, sounds, lights, smoke, and mirrors. It's all fun. But none of it is a necessity.

Your most important tool is still you. The interaction between the presenter and the participants is the reason seminars are so successful and will continue to be. As long as you have a valid message to deliver and you believe in it, so long as you're presenting information that helps your audience, you've got it all.

If your budget doesn't stretch to fancy gizmos right away, that's fine. All you really need is energy and enthusiasm!

Pure Projection

There are all sorts of audiovisual peripherals available to enhance your presentations, ranging from high-tech to low and everything in between. If you want state-of-the-art, go with a multimedia projector (also called a data/video projector). This cool tool connects to your computer, allowing you to show charts, graphs, text, and all those other graphics you produced with your presentation software. You can also project screen shots from your computer so your participants can see them without crowding around you and breathing down your neck—ideal if you'll be doing computer training. And with some units, you can also feed in anything you can put on a CD or DVD for true multimedia pizzaz. Nifty, yes. Inexpensive, no. Expect to spend $1,000 to $3,000 or more.

"Buyer beware!" Larry Smith of National Electrical Seminars in Omaha, Nebraska, says of lower-end LCD projectors. "Generally speaking, the smaller and less costly the projector, the more lights have to be turned off, the shorter the lamp life, the greater the need for sound reinforcement, and the smaller the audience that you can address."

Smart Tip

Tip...

Hotels like to charge extra for everything, even the equipment they normally have on hand, so don't order every audiovisual item available unless you have an actual need for it.

It's Transparent

Much lower on the tech scale, but still perfectly acceptable, is that staple of schoolrooms before the video age: the overhead projector. Expect to pay $100 and up for a portable model to over $500 for a high-end model. Transparencies, on which you can print all sorts of keen graphics with your desktop-publishing software, run $17 and up for a box of 100.

Sliding Around

For seminar groups larger than 20 or 25, you may want to go with the "Our Summer Vacation" favorite of the 1950s—a slide projector and slides. New projectors run from $170 to $700, but if you look around you can probably find a serviceable used one at a garage sale for as little as $20. You can take slides with any camera and have them inexpensively developed at any photo center. Pick up a screen for showing your slides in the $60 to $100 range, or find a used screen to go with the garage-sale projector.

Mark It Up!

If you're doing a fairly intimate seminar, with 10 to 20 people, that modern version of the old chalkboard, the dry-erase marker board, may be all you need to get your points across. Prices for good-quality boards range from about $32 to $325 depending on size and quality. Marker kits, which include erasers and spritz bottles of cleaner, go for $7 to $16 per set.

You could go even more low-tech and use a flip chart, which is basically an oversized pad of paper for scribbling on and is also perfectly acceptable for use in front of groups. Pads run about $26. Then, since it's not exactly ergonomic to hold a 24-inch by 36-inch or larger pad or marker board on your lap while you try to write and talk, you'll want an easel. These handy items range from $15 to $50.

On TV

Stat Fact

According to a recent study by IDC Research, using a multimedia projector enhances audience perception of a presenter by 66 percent.

The hotel or other meeting facility can provide you with TVs or video monitors and videotape players, so don't worry about getting the equipment unless you plan on using your own facility or a community center that doesn't provide them. Plan to spend $250 to $300 for a 25-inch flat-screen television, which can double as a video monitor, and about $150 for a DVD/VCR player.

▲

Stress-Buster

Unless you plan to walk or bicycle to the post office every time you have a package or promotional materials going out, a postage meter is a good idea. Depending on how snazzy you choose to go from among the various models available, you can not only stamp your mail but fold, staple, insert, seal, label, weigh, sort, stack, and wrap it. Whew! The fancier and faster the machine, the more expensive it will be to rent, lease, or purchase.

It used to be that you'd have to lug your postage meter down to the post office and stand in line to get it reset. Not anymore! Now you reset them via phone or computer. What's the cost for all this technology? It depends on what you get, but as a ballpark figure, you can expect to rent a postage meter/electronic scale combo for about $20 to $120 per month.

You can sometimes purchase used equipment from a rental center at rock-bottom prices. Used is OK—but make sure the equipment hasn't been abused. If it's too beat up or worn out, it won't do you any good.

Karaoke Time

Hotels should also be able to set you up with a microphone so you can either lecture to a large audience or perform karaoke classics. If you want to purchase your own, expect to spend $40 to $200 for a wireless model that lets you wander 50 to 200 feet from your lectern as you speak.

Seminar Professional's Office Checklist

Use this handy list as a shopping guide for equipping your office. It's been designed with the one-person home office in mind. If you've got partners, employees, or you just inherited a million dollars from a mysterious foundation with the stipulation that you spend at least half on office equipment, you may want to make modifications.

After you've done your shopping, fill in the purchase price next to each item, add up the total, and you'll have a head start on the Start-Up Costs Worksheet on page 62 in Chapter 4!

❑ Windows XP-based Pentium 4 or Athlon XP PC with
   17-inch or larger LCD screen, modem, and CD-ROM $_____

❑ Laser or inkjet printer   _____

❑ Fax machine or all-in-one printer/fax/copier/scanner   _____

❑ Software:
   Word processing   _____
   Desktop publishing   _____
   Accounting   _____
   Mail order management   _____

❑ Phones, two to three lines with voice mail   _____

❑ Answering machine   _____

❑ Uninterruptible power supply   _____

❑ Surge protector   _____

❑ Calculator   _____

❑ Postage meter/scale   _____

❑ Office supplies (See Mini Shopping List on page 122.)   _____

Not on the Critical List

❑ Digital camera   _____

❑ Scanner   _____

❑ Copier   _____

❑ Desk   _____

❑ Desk chair   _____

❑ Filing cabinet   _____

❑ Bookcase   _____

Total Office Equipment and Furniture Expenditures $_____

The Office Supplies Mini Shopping List

Printer/copier/fax paper $_____

Blank business cards   _____

Letterhead   _____

Matching envelopes   _____

File folders   _____

Address stamp or stickers   _____

Extra printer cartridge   _____

Mouse pad   _____

Miscellaneous office supplies (pencils, paper clips, etc.) _____

Extra fax cartridge   _____

Total Office Supplies Expenditures $_____

Seminar Professional's Special Equipment List

Overhead projector $_____

Multimedia projector   _____

Dry erase marker board   _____

Flip chart   _____

Easel   _____

Slide projector   _____

TV or video monitor   _____

DVD/VCR player   _____

Microphone   _____

Total Special Equipment Expenditures $_____

Sample Office Expenses

Furniture, Equipment, and Supplies	TravelTeach	So Romantic
Computer system	$1,000	$1,500
LCD screen	550	600
Laptop	800	1,000
Printer		800
Fax machine		125
All-in-one printer/fax/scanner/copier	200	
Software	350	1.350
Phone system	80	400
Answering machine	20	
Uninterruptible power supply	125	250
Surge protector	15	60
Calculator	20	70
Copier		600
Desk		800
Desk chair		260
Printer stand		70
File cabinet	60	200
Bookcase	70	70
Printer/copier/fax paper	25	75
Packing/shipping supplies and equipment	25	250
Blank business cards	10	15
Letterhead	23	37
Matching envelopes	43	43
No. 10 blank envelopes	3	12
Address stamp or stickers	10	20
Extra printer cartridge	75	120
Extra fax cartridge		80
Mouse pad	10	30
Dry erase board, markers, and easel	90	246
Used slide projector and screen	40	40
Miscellaneous office supplies	100	200
Total Expenditures	**$3,744**	**$9,323**

8

Command Center
Your Business Location

Every business, like everybody, needs a base—
a safe, secure spot in which to make and implement plans, carry

out operations, and deal with clients and customers. Every busi-

ness—as it grows—also generally reaches the point where it

needs employees to help nurture it to long-term success. In this

chapter, we explore the secrets of choosing the perfect location.

Choosing a Location

As we've explained, one of the perks of running a seminar business is that it lends itself ideally to the homebased entrepreneur. It doesn't require a high-traffic or high-visibility location and doesn't need to be in a trendy part of town. Since your programs take place in rented or client-provided meeting sites, and your other business contacts are virtual (by phone, mail, or internet), you won't need a mahogany-paneled office with a lobby and conference room to impress or entertain clients. The only space requirement is an area large enough for your desk, your chair, your filing cabinets, and perhaps a bookshelf.

The home office is convenient—you couldn't get any closer to your work unless you slept with your computer and your telephone. It's economical—you don't need to spend money on leased space, extra utilities, daily transportation costs, or lunches down at the corner grill.

Working at home is not, however, mandatory. You may want to leave your laundry, your dog, and/or your kids/spouse at home while you go off to an office space that's nice, quiet, clean, and yours alone.

The Home Office

If you choose to be homebased, you can locate your office work space anywhere in the house that's convenient, although ideally, you should have a dedicated office, a room that's reserved just for the business. You could locate this room in a den, a FROG (finished room over garage), the garage itself ,or a spare room. Keep in mind that whatever space you choose will be your work station and command center.

If a dedicated office is not an option, you can also station yourself in a corner of the kitchen or at the dining room table. If you've got a boisterous family, however, a cubbyhole in your bedroom is likely to be much more conducive to quiet, clear thinking than a nook in the family room with the big-screen television blaring at all hours. Also remember that yelling into the phone over cartoon "kerblams" and "pows" will not give your customers confidence in your company's soundness and reliability. Use the worksheet on page 130 to locate and design your home office.

Stat Fact
Respondents in a recent National Speakers Association member survey indicated that 82.2 percent have home offices.

The Tax Man Speaketh

A big advantage to the home office is the ability to wear two hats—to be at home with your family and be at work at the same time. Another advantage is the ability to write it off as a home business. The

IRS will graciously allow you to deduct money from your income taxes if you're using a portion of your home as your income-producing work space. You can deduct a percentage of expenses equivalent to the percentage of space your home office occupies. If, for example, you're using one room in an eight-room house, you can deduct one-eighth of your rent or mortgage plus one-eight of your utility bills.

There is, of course, an if involved here. You can use this deduction if you're using this space solely as your office. If you've turned your spare bedroom into your office and you don't use it for anything but conducting your business, then you qualify. If, however, your office is tucked into a corner of the kitchen and you're still feeding people in there, you don't qualify for the home office deduction (unless you can convince the IRS that you order Chinese every night and the refrigerator is actually a file cabinet).

Alternative Officing

If commercial office space is not your bag, you might consider a more unconventional approach. Rent a house or an apartment (provided you check the zoning laws first). If you already live in an apartment, you may choose to rent another unit in the same building to use as your office. You can walk to work. And the landlord may give you a package deal—or a finder's fee!

You might work out a rental arrangement with a colleague in another type of business who has extra space and needs a little extra income. How about an artist who needs lots of work space but can't quite afford that midtown loft? (Make sure you make arrangements for partition walls or alternate work hours so your ringing phones don't drive him nuts.) Or a newbie real estate agent who'd like help with her office rent in exchange for office space? (Ringing phones in the background make realtors sound good.)

Or rent your own space over a downtown storefront. How about over a coffeehouse or donut shop or bagel bakery? What better incentive to get to work in the morning?

Organized and Efficient

If you prefer to have your coffee and croissant—and your office—in your home, it's important to remember that you're still a professional. Your work quarters, like yourself, should be organized and efficient. If at all possible, designate a separate room with four walls and a door. Aim for pleasant, quiet, well-lit surroundings. You're going to be spending a lot of time in this space, so you want it to be comfortable.

If you can't carve out a dedicated space, by all means take over a corner of another room. But

Bright Idea

Don't come out of the closet. How about going into it? Some homes, especially older ones, have walk-in closets—some with windows—that are large enough to turn into a cozy little office. Just make sure yours has adequate ventilation and light.

▲

consider it your permanent office. Clearing your work materials off the dining room table before meals is a definite drag.

Appropriate a desk or table large enough to hold your computer, keyboard, phone, and pencil holder, stapler, etc. and still have enough room to spread out your working papers. A charming 19th century cherrywood secretary looks great but probably won't allow enough space for your correspondence, files, and you and your computer. Don't skimp on elbow room.

Make sure you have enough space to store currently running and already-tried ads and other promotional materials, as well as files for cur-

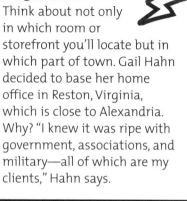

Bright Idea

Think about not only in which room or storefront you'll locate but in which part of town. Gail Hahn decided to base her home office in Reston, Virginia, which is close to Alexandria. Why? "I knew it was ripe with government, associations, and military—all of which are my clients," Hahn says.

rent and potential advertising venues like magazines and newspapers, vendors, clients, and customers. Whether you use the fanciest hanging file folders in mahogany drawers or simple manila ones in cardboard boxes, you must be able to access this information quickly and easily. It's no fun digging through the back of the linen closet or running out to the garage every time somebody calls with a question.

Be sure to print and file hard copies of all e-mail that is sent to you and all missives you send to others. Keeping everything on your computer's hard drive may seem like a swell paper-saving idea, but if your computer crashes, you'll lose everything (including, temporarily, your mind). The same goes for computerized databases of customers and clients.

You will also need space to package your products for shipping. It doesn't matter if it is the kitchen table or a special workstation in your office, so long as there is adequate room to spread out your materials and wrap that package professionally.

Growing Pains

As your business grows, you may decide that it's time to move up to outside or commercial office space. Because the seminar business doesn't rely on client traffic or a prestige address, any area that appeals to you and your pocketbook is up for grabs. Rents in high-traffic areas like malls or trendy downtown shopping areas can be astronomical, so don't set your sights on them. Instead, try going the office/warehouse route in an industrial park.

Don't forget your brochures or other mail-out materials! You'll need easily accessible boxes or shelves where you can keep these items safe, clean, tidy, and ready to go at all times.

Whether your office is an artist's loft, over a bagel bakery, or in an industrial park, you'll need the same basic setup as in a home office, with plenty of room for all those files, plus your desk, chair, minimalist visitors' furniture, and a desk and chair for any employee(s) you may hire.

Bright Idea

If your closet is of the sliding-door/runs-along-one-wall variety, take out the clothes and stash them somewhere. Remove the doors and you've got a dandy office nook.

And let's not forget the electronics. Whether in a home or commercial office, your computer should occupy a place of honor, away from dirt, drafts, and blinding sunlight. Ditto for your printer and fax machine.

In a commercial office, you'll also want that American office altarpiece, the coffee maker, and if you can provide a tidbit or two—a plate of cookies, for example, when you know those rare visitors are arriving—you'll go a long way toward cementing ties. Everyone appreciates a treat!

Of course, with a home office, you can still have coffee and cookies. Goodies are as close as your kitchen. So are all the other joys of home. And after all, isn't that one of the great perks of being able to work from home?

Home Office Worksheet

Use this handy worksheet to locate and design your home office.

List three possible locations in your home for your actual office, a work area for you, your desk, computer, and telephone:

1. _____

2. _____

3. _____

Now make a physical survey of each location.

❑ Are phone and electrical outlets placed so that your equipment can easily access them? Or will you be faced with unsightly, unsafe cords snaking across the carpet?

❑ Measure your space. Will your current desk or table, or the one you have your eye on, fit?

❑ Do you have adequate lighting? If not, can you create or import it?

❑ Is there proper ventilation?

❑ What is the noise factor?

❑ Is there room to spread out your work?

Optional:

❑ How close is the office to the coffee maker? Refrigerator? (This can be either a plus or minus, depending on your current waistline and jitter factor.)

Now list three possible home locations for your inventory:

1. _____

2. _____

3. _____

Now make a survey of each.

❑ Is it climate-controlled? Will you need climate control?

❑ Is there adequate lighting, ventilation, and space for you to easily access your inventory?

❑ Will you need to construct special shelving or other storage? If so, make notes here:

_____

❑ Will you have an adequate, well-lit work space?

❑ Is there room to stash and easily access packing and shipping materials and tools?

9

Your Stage Crew
Finding and Hiring Speakers and Staff

As with any good road show, a lot more people contribute to the success of a seminar than you might think. There's the speaker or presenter, of course, but there are also the unsung folks behind the scenes who book the talent, make the travel arrangements, handle attendees, sell the programs, and perform all sorts of other functions.

In this chapter, we unlock the secrets of who you'll need and how to go about finding them. And we will start with the star of the show, the speaker or presenter.

Finding Presenters

If you plan to act as a promoter rather than a presenter, or if you plan on programs that feature other speakers in addition to yourself, you'll need to locate and negotiate with your talent, which is exactly what we explore in this section. But even if you'll be the only talent, you'll want to read up here. Why? Because it will help you with the business of being the speaker or presenter someone else hires and with knowing what speakers bureaus look for when placing talent for their clients.

Speaker Matchmakers

So how do you go about finding speakers? You could audition friends and neighbors, put an ad in the paper or launch a campaign to track down speakers at every convention in the civilized world. Or—you could contact speakers bureaus, which act as matchmakers of sorts between presenters and promoters or potential clients. Since there are an estimated 600 bureaus around the world, with 80 to 85 percent of them in the United States, you've got plenty to choose from. For a short sampling, see this book's Appendix.

Some bureaus specialize in representing speakers on a single topic, like genealogy, family dynamics, business management, international affairs, or empowerment. Others represent only celebrities or politicians. Most represent a wide variety of professionals.

The speakers you find at bureaus are generally in the top-notch professional class, with proven track records rather than rank beginners. When you surf bureau web sites, you'll find luminaries like Dr. John Gray (the "men are from Mars" man), Henry Kissinger, and Oprah (yes, the TV Oprah), all of whom command staggering fees—from $25,000 to $100,000. But don't let this throw you. There are also lots of speakers who aren't household names (at least not in the homes of people who haven't yet heard them speak), but who turn in a terrific performance at far more reasonable prices—under $2,000.

As a seminar promoter, using a speakers bureau can save you valuable hours. You tell the

Smart Tip

Tip...

If you need to advertise for trainers, seminar professional Denise Dudley advises, go with newspapers in major metropolitan areas. Not only will you find more applicants, but you'll find it much cheaper to fly those based in metro areas—near large airport hubs—to sessions around the country than those who live in less air-accessible areas.

bureau the topics you plan to present, your guidelines (whether speakers should use your script or their own material, for instance), your budget, and when and where the program will take place. The bureau then provides you with a list of potential candidates, sends demo tapes and references, and provides you with the means to contact your chosen few.

And to make a good thing even better, it won't cost you any more to hire a speaker through a bureau than it would to hire the speaker directly, because the bureau gets its commission (typically 25 to 30 percent) from the speaker and not from you.

Finding Your Own Presenters

The downside of speakers bureaus is that they tend to represent people in the higher echelons—those who command the big, big bucks and who are usually booked a year or more in advance. As a newbie, or as the head of a training company who will use the same presenters over and over again, you might do as well or better to find your own speakers.

Denise Dudley finds no shortage of applicants for Mission, Kansas-based SkillPath Seminars. In fact, she says, they always have more trainer hopefuls than they have jobs to fill, a delightful state of affairs she attributes to the company's reputation in the industry.

Unless they have been "pre-approved" by having worked for a reputable competitor, Dudley asks hopeful presenters to send a video and a resume. The resume is then screened to see if there's a match between the candidate's experience and the slot to be filled. If the candidate has been a secretary for 15 years, for instance, she is a better match as a secretarial skills seminar trainer than someone who has been a professor of chemical engineering.

Beware!

Some seminar companies charge prospective presenters for a week of training, deducting their fees from new recruits' first earnings. While this makes for an interesting sideline profit center, it's not ethical.

The New Recruit

When screening videos, the SkillPath staff seeks out one particular quality. "We look for naturalness," Dudley says, "not the Toastmaster training thing where people fling their arms out like they have an affliction. We look for

Champagne Tastes

Most presenters require the hiring entity—corporate client, promoter, or seminar company—to cough up the costs of travel. And the bigger the "name," the more likely it is that they'll have champagne tastes and demand first-class travel. One way to mitigate this seemingly mind-boggling expense is to negotiate an inclusive fee. This means that instead of covering the presenter's exact travel expenses, you agree to a set fee for her to spend as she sees fit. The beauty of this plan is that even if your speaker spends less than you've provided (and tells you so), you've accounted for those travel costs upfront instead of having to pencil them in later.

Another way you can save money on travel expenses for those champagne-taste types who want first-class air fare is to ask if they've got frequent flier miles saved up. The answer will probably be yes because these people fly a lot. Then ask if they'd be willing to use those miles on an upgrade to first-class from the coach ticket you'll pay for. They just might say yes.

Keep in mind that you don't have to pay first-class for anybody—it's your choice, and your judgment call if you feel you might lose a top-notch speaker over the issue.

people who can be real—they're the ones who can hold an audience for six hours." The content of the video isn't that important; it's the natural quality they want to see shine through. Many applicants send in hourlong tapes done in their living rooms, which is fine. "But we can tell in ten minutes," Dudley relates.

Once the applicant passes the resume/video test, she's flown in for an interview at the company's expense. Four of five people auditioned are hired on the spot—that's how important the resume and video are. The new recruit is then sent home with a set of training materials: a video of the program she'll do performed by another trainer and various resource books. Then she's brought back for a run-through with the company staff standing in as participants. If she doesn't pass with flying colors, she's sent back for more self-training. Says Dudley, "We don't take people before they're ready."

On the Road

SkillPath pays trainers an average of $300 per day, plus a sliding scale of commissions on all product sales—which can easily come to another $300 per seminar. Trainers devote different amounts of time to giving seminars, depending on their own preferences. The only condition is that they each give the firm two weeks of five contiguous days per month. This makes it easier to schedule seminars in connecting cities, like Chicago one day, Milwaukee the next, and Madison the next. The company pays trainers' travel expenses and gives them a per diem or daily allowance of $40 while they're on the road to cover meals, taxis, tips, and all the sundry costs that demand attention from a traveler's pocketbook.

Mr. Right

As Dudley has discovered, a speaker can present you with a hip resume, terrific references and a brilliant brochure, but it's what he does in front of an audience that counts. That's why you want to see his demo video before you engage him.

Ideally, you should also get an up-close-and-personal version of his presentation skills to go along with the video. If you can't attend a meeting at which he's featured, try to schedule a personal interview. The way a person presents himself in an interview can speak volumes about his style and professionalism. And it can provide excellent clues as to whether he's the Mr. Right for your target audience.

Besides getting a general feel for your speaker—feeling out whether he's a stuffed shirt and a bore or a wise, wonderful and witty expert on his chosen topic—there are several things you'll want to ask during the interview. We've given you a head start with the worksheet starting on page 142. Make copies to use for your interviews, or modify it to incorporate anything that's germane to the programs you're designing.

Timing Is Everything

Be sure to ask about the length of time a speaker usually gives a topic and how long her last five or 10 speeches have been. This is important because it's more difficult to be effective in 30 to 45 minutes than in two to four hours. With a very short time span, it's a challenge to leave an audience with the impression that they've been given tangible tools to work with. On the other hand, it takes a special person to keep things going for four to six hours or more, even with breaks, and still be effective.

Examine your seminar format and your seminar material and decide how much time your speaker will need. Will you do better to have several speakers presenting short formats, a main speaker with two "guests," or a single speaker presenting a long program? Professional presenters who've seen it all can give you good advice during the interview process, so don't be afraid to ask.

▲

Speaking of Agreements . . .

Once you have chosen your dream speaker and negotiated fees and expenses, you'll need to draw up an agreement, a legal document outlining the obligations of all parties involved in the planned engagement—the seminar promoter, the speakers bureau, and the speaker. Draw up a draft of your agreement and then have your attorney review it to make sure you haven't overlooked or misrepresented any aspect. Once you've got a good boilerplate document, you should be able to make new ones for each program, changing the names, dates, fees, and other particulars as necessary.

Include the following:

- the names and addresses of the promoter or company, presenter, and speaker
- the date, time, and duration of the program
- expected number of participants, if available
- suggested dress or dress code
- travel arrangements, including who makes them, who pays for what, and when it is paid
- presenter's fee, including the method, amounts and times of payment
- speakers bureau fee, if applicable
- whether the presenter will be allowed to sell products; if so, who will pay for inventory, who will garner the proceeds and in what percentages? (Many speakers bureaus collect commissions on product sales in addition to the standard commissions on engagement fees.)
- a reminder of the presenter's status as an independent contractor rather than as an employee
- your rights as a promoter in case the speaker doesn't make the seminar; this happens rarely, but occasionally presenters fall prey to unprovoked attacks by severe kamikaze flu viruses, hurricane-delayed flights, or unforeseen emergencies.

> **Stat Fact**
> According to a recent National Speakers Association survey, the largest percentage of respondents (45.6 percent) have no staff, 29.1 percent (the next largest percentage of respondents) count only one employee, and only 2.1 percent have between 6 and 10 employees.

Office and On-Site Employees

Depending on how much growth you envision for your business, you may never need employees. Or you may expand to the point where you can't do everything yourself—the point where you'll need to consider getting assistance. Employees are another of those funny facts of life that seem to bring with them as many cons as pros. When you hire help, you're not a swinging single anymore. You've got responsibilities. Suddenly there's payroll to be met, workers' compensation insurance to be paid, and state and federal employee taxes to be paid. And work to be delegated.

Some people are born employers, finding it easy to teach someone else the ropes and then hand over the reins. Others never feel quite comfortable telling someone else what to do or how to do it.

Bright Idea

Nance Cheifetz of Sense of Delight in Novato, California, turned the tables on the office help idea and signed on for a temporary stint as a part-time marketing assistant for a speakers bureau. By doing so, she learned what clients were looking for and also—when appropriate—promoted herself!

One of the many perks of the seminar business is that you can accomplish a great deal without ever hiring anyone. You can easily start out as a one-man band, handling all the tasks of your fledgling company yourself. You won't need help immediately. But as your company flourishes, you may one day find that you need a) more hours in a day, b) to make great strides in the field of cloning, or c) to hire help.

SkillPath boasts a staff of 300 administrative employees. Reston, Virginia-based Fun*cilitators, on the other hand, is a one-person business and intends to stay that way.

Independent Thought

So how do you find that pair of hands, attached to a body and a brain capable of independent thought? Take a look at the key words here: independent thought. Your first employee, your administrator, will know more about your business than anybody else except you and your partners (if you have any). So you want someone you can trust. And since your administrator will hold down the fort alone while you're on the road, you want someone who can not only be your spare brain to keep things humming in your absence but can act intelligently in a crisis.

Seek out an assistant with a background in customer service, marketing, or general office administration. Place an ad in your local paper and don't forget to network. Word-of-mouth referrals are often a terrific way to find that gem of an employee.

"I'm the chief bottle washer and CEO," owner Gail Hahn says, "and I handle everything from travel plans to accounting to graphic design of my marketing materials. I have a CPA for annual taxes and advice, and I outsource my webmaster and some data input of business cards and mailing lists."

Smart Tip

If you plan to base your office at home, be sure to update your homeowners' or renters' insurance policy for all your computer and other equipment, especially if you purchase anything new.

Being a one-woman band is perfect for Hahn. "It's all I want to do," she explains. "I don't want to work more than that. A seminar takes time to prepare and time to follow up." If success forces too much growth, she plans to force it right back—she'd raise her fees, some clients would drop out, and she'd get back to a manageably sized company.

Nance Cheifetz of Sense of Delight in Novato, California, shares the same philosophy. "I don't have a staff," she says. "My goal is never to have one. I don't want an organization that I have to manage."

Larry Smith of National Electrical Seminars has one part-time employee who's been with him since his Omaha, Nebraska-based company's inception. "She manages the office," he says, "does some bookkeeping, answers the phone, and does some marketing.

"I've been getting pressure to hire and train other presenters," the former fire and accident investigator adds, "which I may do in time. For the present, I am content to conduct all seminars."

Dr. Jerry Old has one loyal staff member at his Shawnee, Kansas, business. "I have a secretary, receptionist, coach, counselor, and great cheerleader—who I am fortunate to be married to—named Kristi," he says. "She works for free, so I have no employees."

The Office Administrator

You may be able to manage without an office administrator when you start your business, but unless—like Old—you've got built-in help, you may soon find that you need assistance. It's up to you to make initial contacts with corporate and association clients, speakers bureaus, speakers, hotels and other sites, printers, video and audio duping services, salespeople, and the media. Whew! Having another pair of hands to help juggle all these elements can be critical to your company's growth.

You'll want someone who's willing and able to handle many facets of your business. Take a look at this list of tasks your administrator can and should help to take off your hands:

- answer phones
- send out agreements

- coordinate travel arrangements
- coordinate meeting facility arrangements
- pre-screen presenters' resumes and videos
- outline topics for future seminars
- supervise the collection of seminar enrollment fees
- send out press releases

> **Smart Tip** Tip...
>
> Don't forget that your administrator will need writing, word-processing, and database-management skills. Add computer literacy to your list.

The Sales Staff

As your company grows, you may want to hire a sales staff. Most sales reps are active members of lots of professional organizations, which gives them an automatic in to some powerful target markets. They can also market your less-expensive offerings to large and small associations, clubs, and centers throughout the country. And they can target large and small businesses in cities where your seminars will be held and sell tickets in blocks.

Don't forget that salespeople themselves make terrific audiences for public seminars on sales-oriented topics, so your reps can make cold calls to surrounding businesses, telling them about the sales-boosting motivation and skills training your seminars offer. Then, in the old "tell two friends who'll tell two friends" tradition, your reps can network with other salespeople and get them to convince their sales managers to send them to your events.

Depending on the number of seminars you'll host each year, you'll need to decide whether to hire a sales associate or to contract with a professional sales rep who serves many clients. If you take on your very own sales rep, you'll pay a base salary plus commissions. If you outsource your sales staff, you'll pay strictly on commission—and you may want to develop a commission structure that rewards both large group and individual sales.

The Marketing Department

It takes more than a sales whiz to sell seminars. It also takes talent—in the form of marketing smarts, copywriting panache, and graphic design genius to make those brochures and other sales materials sing. As your business grows, you may want to take on a marketing director or a copywriting and graphics guru to help plan new campaigns and keep the old ones selling strong.

Since most of your promotions will take the form of direct-mail advertising, you'll want a person with a background in direct mail—and even better, if possible, one with seminar promotion experience. And just as when you engage presenters, you'll want to see the results of your applicants' work, so be sure to ask for a number of samples.

Insuring Your Gems

Once you find those gems of employees, you'll need to think about caring for them. Workers' compensation insurance laws vary from state to state; check with your insurance agent for details in your area. Workers' comp covers you for any illness or injury your employees might incur, from a paper cut gone septic or a back injury from lifting heavy boxes to radiation poisoning from close contact with the computer terminal.

Although your employee may be working in your home, your homeowners' insurance probably won't pay for a problem incurred there on the grounds that it's actually a workers' compensation case. Rather than making yourself a nervous wreck over all this (incurring your own mental health claim), check with your insurance agent and then make an informed decision.

Temporary Seminar Help

Besides the employees who will work with you on a regular basis at your home base, you may also want to engage temporary assistants to work the actual seminars—which is less expensive than flying your office staff from, say, Sioux City, Iowa, to work a program in Poughkeepsie, New York. These people can include ushers, seminar assistants, and cashiers to work the product table. If you're hosting a seminar with a big-name celebrity who'll attract a large crowd, you might want to hire a security guard.

Seminar Assistants

Seminar assistants, also called hosts and hostesses or program managers, handle the basic but important tasks of greeting participants, handing out name tags and workbooks, helping people find their seats, collecting enrollment fees, and answering general questions about the day's events. If you'll schedule seminars fairly routinely in a particular city, this is a wonderful job for people who only want to work a few days a month, like stay-at-home moms, retired people, or freelance writers and other artistic types with flexible schedules.

Bright Idea

When Novato, California's, Nance Cheifetz needs an assistant for an out-of-town event, she sometimes finds one in her client's own employee pool. "I might ask the client if they want to save some money and find some volunteers to help out with the program," she says. "It actually works out."

You can hire these people through temporary help agencies in your target city or by placing ads in those cities' local newspapers. The big plus to the temporary agency method is that the agency does all the screening and pays all taxes and insurance. Basically, all you have to do is put in an order and be on-site to receive your assistants. The downside is that because the agency pays those taxes and insurance (and also, funnily enough, pencils in a profit for itself), you'll pay

Bright Idea

Offer students free seminar admission in exchange for ushering duties. You get needed help, and they get attendance at a program they might otherwise not be able to afford.

more for an agency-acquired assistant than you would if you found her on your own. Also, agencies are sometimes so anxious to fill your order that they send out people who don't actually meet your requirements.

If you run ads yourself, you pick and choose, but you'll also have to be available to meet applicants. You can arrange to do this when you first visit a new city so you've got your assistants already online for your next seminar, or you might have them send resumes and conduct telephone interviews before the seminar.

Another option—and a good one—is to use your seminars to solicit assistants. "We used to put a little flier out on the table that said, 'Are You Interested in Being a Program Manager? Or Do You Know Someone Who Would Be?'" Denise Dudley says. "Most of the time, that would do it. People took home that flier, and they had a retired mom who would just love to be a hostess, and we heard from them and acquired them that way." These program managers worked out so well that SkillPath now rarely needs to do any new hiring. They simply call on the experienced pros they've already used in each city. "In cities like Phoenix, where we do a lot of seminars," Dudley explains, "we have one or two people who do the SkillPath seminars whenever we come to town and want to do them. In cities that we don't visit as often, we might call on any number of people who've done SkillPath seminars before. So we hardly ever have to put those fliers out."

Ushers and Security

High school and college kids make terrific ushers. They're not looking for a tremendous amount of prestige, the part-time hours suit them fine, and they don't expect a king's ransom as wages. Contact career centers and have them post ads for you.

Security guards are not people you'll need at most events. Unless you're featuring Jimmy Carter, Madonna, or the Pope, you probably don't need to worry about this issue at all. If the need arises, however, the hotel, arena or other facility should be able to provide security. If not, you'll find a number of reputable security service agencies in the Yellow Pages.

Speaker Interview Worksheet

Make your speaker candidate comfortable. Explain a little about your concept for the program and what you have in mind for his part in it. Then ask these pertinent questions and make notes in the spaces provided.

1. What is your experience with this topic and the type of audience or partici- pants we'll be working with? _____

    _____

    _____

    _____

2. Tell me about similar engagements you've had in the past two years. What did you feel was particularly successful about them? What, if anything, would you do differently this time? _____

    _____

    _____

    _____

3. What can you bring to this program that no one else could? _____

    _____

    _____

4. What will you do to customize your speech or workshop for this audience?

    _____

    _____

5. What length do you suggest for your speech or workshop? _____

    _____

    If shorter or longer than what you had in mind, ask this: Can you shorten or lengthen it by _____ (amount)?

6. What do you feel is the greatest challenge in working with this type of audi- ence or participants and why?

    _____

    _____

Speaker Interview Worksheet, continued

7. What do you feel is the greatest reward and why?

_____

_____

8. What suggestions can you make about the overall format and tone of the program?

_____

_____

9. Would you want to sell products after the program? (*If yes, and if you want products sold, you can discuss it here. If not, ask if your candidate would have a problem not selling products.*)

_____

_____

10. We're a young and dynamic company with great potential. But since we're young—and also smart—we carefully budget our seminars. Let's discuss your fees.

_____

_____

11. Please provide me with five recent references from clients or promoters.

_____

_____

_____

_____

_____

Marquee
Magic, Part 1
Direct-Mail
Advertising

In this chapter we explore one of the most fun, exciting, and creative—and most demanding—parts of the seminar business, advertising and promotion. After all, no matter how thrilling, informative, life-affirming, or business-rescuing your seminars are, nobody's going to know about them unless you advertise. As a seminar professional, a great deal of your resources will go into designing and implementing advertising campaigns to take your sales to the limits and beyond.

Unless your featured presenter is somebody really big like Elvis ("direct from the Otherworld!"), you can't rely on a marquee blazing with neon and arc lights, so you'll need to devise other methods of getting the word out. Your best bets are direct mail, personal contact, and word-of-mouth. Venues like radio, television, magazines, and newspapers—which can work wonders for other types of entrepreneurs—don't make much of a dent on the psyches of potential seminar participants.

You can make radio, TV, and magazines terrific promotional tools, but not in the way you might think. In the next two chapters, we'll tell you how and more, as we explore the secrets of advertising and promotion for fun and profit. Yes, really! It can be a lot of fun—so let's get going!

Direct Mail

"We almost exclusively use direct mail," says Denise Dudley of SkillPath's advertising methods. "Our most successful advertising for our public seminars," Larry Smith of National Electrical Seminars concurs, "is direct mail." Most seminar professionals agree that it's the method of choice for advertising to unsolicited sources, those who haven't already contacted you and indicated interest. What exactly is direct mail? It's another way of saying mail order, and it can take the form of sales letters, brochures, postcards, or any other printed material you send winging into the mailboxes of potential seminar customers.

The Dossier

Direct-mail advertising can be extremely effective, but it's also expensive. By the time you pay for the paper, envelopes, printing, and postage for a major campaign, you've spent thousands of dollars. So before you pop those 50,000 sales pieces in the mail, make sure you've thoroughly considered what it is that your niche market wants or needs and how your seminars will satisfy that desire or need.

The first thing to do when you start your advertising campaign is to take a figurative step back. Revisit your market research. Like a top-secret government organization targeting sectors

Tip...

Smart Tip
There are several mail order associations that can be of tremendous assistance in your direct-marketing efforts. (We particularly recommend the National Mail Order Association in Minneapolis.) Check out this book's Appendix for these associations' contact information.

of the public, you too have a "dossier" you've put together on your potential participants. Your dossier should include the following:

- Who are my potential customers?
- How many are there?
- Where are they located?
- Where do they now find the information I want to provide?
- What can I offer that they're not already getting from this other source?
- How can I persuade them to attend my seminars?

Look over the answers to these questions; then ask yourself some more:

- What knowledge and skills do I offer?
- What image do I want to project?
- How do I compare with my competition and how can I be better?

Once you've answered these critical questions and you know exactly who you're targeting, with what, and why, it's time to devise your direct-mail piece.

Direct-Mail Dazzle

You can use any direct-mail format that works for you, from a letter introducing yourself and describing your seminars to a one-page flier to a multipage brochure. Denise Dudley's Mission, Kansas-based SkillPath sends brochures to potential new customers and letters to past participants; Larry Smith relies on brochures; and Dr. Jerry Old sends fliers for his Shawnee, Kansas, business's occasional direct-mail forays.

Experimentation, testing, and—always, always—market research will tell you which format is the best for your company. We're going to talk here about brochures because they're the format you'll probably want to start off with, but you can—and should—apply these same success secrets and tips to any other direct-mail piece you design.

The "Wow!" Brochure

What should your brochure look like? That depends on the image of your company and—just as in choosing a hotel site—what will appeal to your target market.

"We use a very simple, plain brochure," says Larry Smith, the Omaha, Nebraska-based electrical trainer. "It folds to letter size. Our logo is on the front. We have that logo on several items—the most important is on the back of our

Bright Idea

Check into issues of mail order-oriented magazines like *Catalog Age* and *Target Marketing* for lots of direct-mail tips and tricks. You'll find contact information in this book's Appendix.

table cards. A seminar participant can't avoid getting the logo burned into his or her brain. It clicks on future mailings.

"Keeping the brochure simple," Smith relates, "not only keeps the costs down but appeals to our clientele—an expensive color brochure would probably convey that we make too much money!"

As Larry has discovered, you don't have to go with an expensive glossy, four-color masterpiece. Choose a light-colored card stock and one or two bold, professional colors for your text. With the bounty of desktop-publishing software out there, you can choose from a dazzling array of fonts, borders, and line art to jazz up your text. But don't sacrifice clarity for cutesiness. A few graphics go a long way.

You can design your brochure so that it's the tidy size of a No. 10 (business-size) envelope. See the sample on page 159. Or you can try a size that will make it stand out from all the other No. 10 envelopes in the mailbox. How about 8 inches by 5 inches? Choose whatever size suits your layout and your budget. But think about how you feel when you see that odd-sized envelope in your daily handful of mailbox bills and clutter. Don't you automatically think, "Wow! Something special!" and open it first?

Brochure Brilliance

Once you've decided on the basics, take these tips into consideration:

- *Mug shot not.* People like to see who and what they're spending their money on, so add photos of yourself or your presenter (not your driver's license mug shot but a professional-quality picture). Make sure the photos are sharp and clear.

- *Name power.* If you use a celebrity, emphasize his name, as in "VICTOR FRANKENSTEIN tells you how to breathe new life into your career." If he's not (yet) a star, emphasize the seminar's title and content, as in "LEARN TO BREATHE NEW LIFE INTO YOUR CAREER with Frankenstein Seminars' Powerful 10-Step Program for Becoming a Monster Manager."

- *Tempt with teasers.* Tease your potential customer with highlights of your seminar's content, like this:

  1. Unlocking the secrets of creativity
  2. The importance of seeing things through new eyes
  3. How to find your inner strengths
  4. Time-saving strategies for dealing with customers

> **Tip...**
>
> **Smart Tip**
>
> Explain why you are—or your presenter is—superbly qualified to lead this program. If you're training home inspectors and you've been a home inspector for 10 years or a county building inspector for 20 years, say so.

Think like a movie theater coming attraction or the blurb on the back of a bestselling book. Leave your customer eager to hear the details—which he can only do by signing up!

- *Benefiting from benefits.* Explain the benefits of your seminar, the harvest your customer will reap from attending, as in "Increase your productivity. Dissolve that daily stress overdose and learn to have fun! Gain financial security by freeing your mind to create instead of worry."

> **Tip...**

Smart Tip

Have a professional proofreader scan your brochure. Sometimes it's almost impossible to detect minor typos in your own work, and computer program spelling and grammar checkers, while helpful, can sometimes interpret things in a strange fashion.

- *Details, details.* Don't forget the details! Make sure you explain where and when your seminar will be held and how much it costs.

- *Discounts and freebies.* Tempt them further with discounts for seniors, spouses, students, or groups, or with freebies like autographed books, special planning calendars, glow-in-the-dark neck bolts (Frankenstein seminars only), or some other back-of-the-room (BOR) product.

- *Contact.* Put your address and phone number where they're easy to see and read. Don't forget your web site and e-mail addresses. More and more people like the ease of ordering—and enrolling—online. "The number of registrations that come in across the internet has risen astronomically," Smith says.

- *Drum roll to enroll.* Include your enrollment form—the really important part!

- *The rules.* Add in any rules or restrictions, such as prohibited taping devices or smoking, or that all tickets must be purchased in advance. Clarify your refund or credit policy.

A Paper You

Your brochure is the paper version of you—a sort of rudimentary hologram (like Princess Leia in Star Wars!) that lands on your prospective customer's desk or kitchen table and says, "Pay attention! I've got just what you need!"

> **Tip...**

Smart Tip

If you're doing a continuing education seminar, remind your prospects that the seminar and associated travel, lodging, and meal expenses are tax-deductible.

Since most people today are flooded with direct mail pieces, yours needs to leap off the desk or table and instantly capture your potential client's attention so that she'll pick it up instead of tossing it aside. Then, when she does pick it up, it must keep her attention so she'll read it

Don't Be Shy

OK, you're thinking, I know I should include testimonials in my advertising, but how do I get them? There are several ways, all beginning with the word "ask"—just as you do on your evaluation forms. When customers write to compliment you on your products, services, or company, ask if you can use that compliment as a testimonial. When they call with a compliment, ask if you can write out what they've said and send it to them for a signature. Don't be shy. The customer is helping you, but at the same time you're giving him that little spot in the limelight. And you're forging a relationship.

What if you're a brand-new newbie and you haven't done a seminar from which to get testimonials? Ask friends or colleagues for quotes on things you've done to help them that are related to your seminar topic. If, for example, you'll be giving workshops on web site design for small businesses, you might try for something like this: Wally Beaver knows internet marketing inside and out. He taught me to design my own web site, and because of it my business has soared. –June Ward, graphic designer. It's a bona fide testimonial and relates directly to the seminar you'll present but doesn't say "seminar." Instead, it points out your expertise and the benefit to the potential customer, which is (you knew it!) increased business and profits.

through. Besides interest and attention, the main thing to aim for in your brochure is the sense that you're writing to her personally with the solution to her personal problem or her company's specific problem. Why? You remember: because that's what your seminar is designed to do—problem-solve.

The Hook

If this sounds daunting, try reading all those direct-mail pieces that land in your mailbox. The best ones to study, of course, are those that pitch seminars, but carefully examine all of them—even those that are selling summer vacations or winter sweaters. What do they have in common? For one thing, they start off with something that immediately hooks your attention. Maybe it's a description of the offer, enticing you to read on with tidbits of the information you'll get when you buy that seminar enrollment or book or newsletter. Maybe it's a description of the benefits of having attended the seminar, like more self-confidence or better customer service or greater financial security.

Try the same approaches with your brochure. Experiment until you hit on something that sounds good to you and matches your particular topic.

Beware!
Remember that if you use testimonials, they must be from real people who have given their permission to use their comments.

Then go on to the body of the brochure. Again, analyze the ones you've received. What makes them work? Notice that they spend a lot of time describing the seminar's benefits. You'll want to do the same thing. Emphasize the benefits of your programs throughout your body copy, repeating those benefits as often as you can using different descriptions so they stick in your customer's mind.

If you've got testimonials, use them, too. They lend credibility to your programs and your company, and they add another dimension to your copy by showing that it's not just you who thinks your seminars are great—it's real people just like your prospect.

After the main body of your brochure, tell your customer what she needs to do to sign up for your seminar. Put in a convenient order form that she can send back, or make your phone number is large and legible so she can call and order the program if she'd prefer. If you're offering a discount with a time element, this is the place to mention it.

Try putting in a time element like "Order by June 14th to receive your 20 percent discount on the normal seminar price of $99," or "Order by June 14th to receive your free seminar companion book." This lights a fire under your customer—she won't want to put off ordering because she'll lose out on the discount or freebie.

The Personal Touch

Check out the brochure starting on page 159. Then check out these sales tips:

- *Grab that prospect's attention.* Remember to relate it directly to your seminar and how it will benefit him.

- *Use time-proven winning words like "secret" and "free."* Everybody wants to know a secret, and everybody wants something for free! Like what? How about something like: Discover the secrets to living rich while investing most of your income! Or Free fat-burning calculator when you enroll in our high-energy, low-fat cookery seminar!

- *Where you have space, try for headlines of ten or more words—longer sells better than shorter.*

Bright Idea
If you don't feel you've got the right copywriting stuff and you can't afford to hire a professional, hire a college student majoring in advertising to take over your brochure-designing duties. You'll benefit from her fresh ideas, and she'll benefit from the resume- favorable experience. Who knows? As your company grows, you might even take her on as a full-time employee.

The Participation Effect

Another of the quirky things about direct mail (which goes with another of the quirky things about human nature) is that people are far more likely to respond to an offer for which they have to actively do something than one for which they do nothing. In other words, people like direct-mail offers in which they're asked, for example, to paste a "yes" or "no" sticker on the reply card. That's why all those Publishers Clearing House packets are full of stickers, reply cards, and tear-offs. They work. Call it the participation effect.

Of course, these gimmicks cost money, but if you can afford them—and if they fit your company style—by all means use them. If not, think how else you might incorporate the same idea into your enrollment form. If you're offering a free gift with enrollment, for instance, you might let them choose between an audiotape or a book by checking a box on your form.

Then, make sure your form is clear, easy to understand and easy to fill out. Check out the sample self-mailer on page 161.

- *Don't write for thousands of prospective customers—write to just one, as though you're speaking to him personally.*
- *Save the flowery prose for that poetry contest.* Instead, use everyday language for the average person.
- *Don't focus only on the features of your seminars—describe the benefits.*
- *Try indented paragraphs, underlined words, and two colors—they pack more of a punch and outpull plain text.*
- *But—use gimmicks like boldface type, underlining, and italics sparingly.* If you use them too much, they become annoying instead of intriguing.
- *Keep your materials clear, clean and free of grammar and style errors.* Have someone you trust as a spelling, punctuation, and grammar star check your work before you commit to a print run.
- *Relax and enjoy yourself.* Have fun!

Sure-Fire Techniques

OK, we've seen what direct mail looks like and how to design your own for optimum effect. Now let's review the sure-fire techniques for winning customers:

- *Give away freebies with prompt enrollment.* Remember—everybody likes to have something for free. Everybody likes a gift. Depending on your style, budget, and target market, you can give away something substantial (but inexpensive) or a mere trinket. If your seminars focus on foreign travel, how about a money conversion table, a French phrase book, or a copy of your own autographed book? If you choose something your customers will use often, and then imprint it with your company name, you'll have given away not only a gift but free advertising for yourself.

Smart Tip Tip...

Make it easy for prospects to order. Explain that they can enroll by mail, phone, or fax (or your web site, if you're set up for it) and that they can pay by check or credit card.

• *Offer a money-back guarantee.* When prospective customers see that you stand behind the "goods" you promise to deliver, you help them over the hurdle of sending their money to someone they don't know for something they haven't actually received (and which—except for freebies, workbooks, or BOR products—isn't even something tangible they can hold in their hands). When you offer that guarantee, use strengthening words like "unconditional" or "no questions asked" to show that you're serious about your offer. And don't forget that if you offer a money-back guarantee, you have to honor it—it's the law.

Accentuate the Positive

Don't get confused about the difference between the features and benefits of your seminar—it's the latter you want to sell. The features of your program would be, for example, an intensive two-day workshop with a leading romance writer, take-home workbooks for each participant, and a special half-day workshop with a romance novels editor. This is good.

But as far as your prospective customer is concerned, your workshop could be led by an auto mechanic and a dentist for all the good it will do—unless you stress the benefits. As the old song says, accentuate the positive, the things that will make a significant positive change in the customer's life as a writer of romances. Emphasize insider knowledge of what editors are looking for, increased creativity, improved productivity, and personal empowerment and motivation (no more writer's block).

When you write your copy, you should describe the features, but just as—or more—important is telling your customers about the benefits, because these, after all, are the reasons they buy.

- *Time-date your offers.* Say something like "If you respond within the next 30 days, you'll receive a free _____" or "This offer is good only through _____." This encourages your customers to enroll now instead of in the nebulous future. And when you combine a time-dated offer with a money-back guarantee, you will increase your responses.

- *Write riveting headlines.* Your brochure must compete with those scads of others crammed in your customers' mailboxes. Your pitch can be terrific and your programs, products, and price can be unbeatable, but if you don't catch their eyes with your opening salvo—your headline—they're never going to know how special your offer is. Winning headlines generally come in three basic styles: the ego appeal, as in "you have been selected" or "you're invited"; the greed appeal, as in "free gift"; and the news

Bright Idea

The brochure is a terrific opportunity to sell BOR products. Pitch them while you pitch the seminar—people who can't make your program due to time or financial constraints may be delighted to buy your books and tapes.

Lists Galore

Want a sample of just how many lists are out there and how selective they can be? Check out these offerings from various list owners or brokers who advertised in just one recent issue of *Catalog Age* magazine:

- ○ gardeners
- ○ home workshop enthusiasts
- ○ cat and dog owners
- ○ hikers and campers
- ○ boating enthusiasts
- ○ video producers
- ○ medical professionals
- ○ health-conscious Hispanics
- ○ amateur and professional jewelers
- ○ high-end travelers (those who spend mucho dinero)
- ○ career women
- ○ offshore fishermen

appeal, as in "a new discovery." Penning your headline before your copy will help you focus on what basic need or desire your product satisfies and what appeal your copy should make.

- *Offer testimonials from satisfied customers, using real first and last names and real hometowns.* If you use only initials or first names, your true-life kudos can look invented. Add a client list to your brochure as soon as possible. A list of satisfied clients adds to your credibility and helps prospects feel they're making the right choice.

- *Accent with artwork.* Illustrations and photos attract attention. If you use a caption under a picture, make sure it has sales value—people read captions even when they don't have time to read the rest of the piece.

- *Give them a kick with catchwords.* Certain words trigger emotional responses—some of the most persuasive in the language, especially when it comes to advertising materials, are "new," "free," "how to," "love," and "discover." Guess which two are the absolute tops in advertising? New and free!

- *Help customers respond quickly.* Accept credit cards and toll-free calls. It's much easier for your customer to fill in a credit card number on a form or call and give it to you over the phone than to sit down and write out a check.

- *Remember the participation effect.* Give your customers plenty to look at, lots to read, and if possible, something to stick, paste, tear off, or insert. If you can't afford these gimmicks, consider something like the seemingly handwritten note that implores the customer to "Read this only if you've decided not to attend."

I Love Mailing Lists

That said, let's revisit mailing lists. You already know a bit, but there's lots more. A mailing list can make or break a direct-mail campaign, and a good list can be worth more than double your ad budget.

You can target your audience more effectively with a mailing list than with any other medium. Say you decide to go with an alternative and advertise on television. We don't recommend it, but for the sake of making a point, we'll do it anyway. You might choose *I Love Lucy* or *The X-Files* reruns or the *Tonight Show*. Although each will have its demographic profile, you'll get a fairly indiscriminate selection of viewers. You have no way of knowing if they're sales managers, executives who travel overseas, romance authors, or maximum security prison inmates who couldn't attend one of your seminars even if it were free.

Ah, but when you rent a mailing list, you've got your audience targeted to a T. You can choose Midwestern women who've bought bridal magazines (for plan-your-own-wedding seminars) or Northeastern men who buy woodworking tools and earn more

▲

The Formula

Like any good mad scientist, the seminar professional also has a magic formula—for working with lists. That formula is RFM, with R for recency, F for frequency, and M for money. What this actually means is this: How recently have the people on the list ordered a seminar by mail, how frequently do they order, and how much do they spend?

Besides the all-important RFM factor, demographics are crucial in choosing your list. You need to consider income, age, gender, education, type of residence, occupation, and use of credit cards in making purchases. If you're selling romance-writing seminars, you'd probably choose a girls-only list, because most men wouldn't be interested. Got it? Good.

Another list selection factor is psychographics. This is the categorization of people by psychological profile. Political conservatives, for instance, are more likely to be hunters than people on the liberal left. So if you're selling duck-hunting seminars, you might try mailing to Republicans. If a list owner or broker says he's got a psychographic profile, ask for it. Check out the ones listed to see if they match your prospective buyers.

Yet another factor to consider is who else has been renting the same list and how often. This can tell you who your competition is and how successful they've been with it. If you've got employee motivation workshops and you find that another employee training company has rented the same list four times in the past year, you can figure they're having good luck with it, which means you probably will, too.

than $50,000 per year (for build-your-own-home workshops), or companies in the Southwest that employ more than 2,000 people (for customer service seminars).

Common Threads

In the mailing list world, there are two types of lists: the compiled list and the buyer or response list. A compiled list is made up of people with the common thread of a group or organization—for example, members of alumni organizations or car clubs, members of professional organizations from doctors to contractors, or even people who have attended different types of seminars or workshops. A compiled list can also be made up of people with certain demographic characteristics in common—those who live in Manhattan or make more than $30,000 per year or are between 45 and 70 years old. You get the picture. The main point to remember with compiled lists is that unless you rent a list that comprises previous seminar attendees, you can't know that those doctors, contractors, or car aficionados have ever purchased seminar tickets or are likely to.

Now, the other type of list—the buyer list—is the one you want to shoot for. Why? Because the people on the list are already known seminar participants. They might be buyers of gourmet cooking workshops or dog training seminars or employee motivation programs, but the main idea here is that since they've already purchased a seminar similar to yours, they're likely to purchase yours as well.

> **Tip...**
>
> **Smart Tip**
> It's always wise to test your list—before you send out 50,000 brochures to every name on the list, rent 5,000 names, send your mailing, and see what sort of response you get.

This may not be the case with people on compiled lists. This doesn't mean you should never use compiled lists. It does mean, though, that you should use them carefully. Your list broker is experienced at this sort of thing, so let him advise you on what's best for your particular situation.

Mailing List Fever

Where exactly do you get your mailing lists?

- Rent them from any number of list brokers, which you'll find in your local Yellow Pages under "Advertising—Direct Mail" or within the pages of direct-marketing magazines like *Catalog Age* and *Target Marketing*. (To get you started, we've provided the names of a few mailing list brokers in our Appendix.)

- Rent or swap lists directly from your competition (yes! they will often share), other seminar companies engaged in selling programs to similar target markets.

- Rent directly from associations whose members fit your target market.

- Buy lists from a competitor who's gone out of business (doesn't happen often but is worth keeping an eye out for).

- Build up your own list in all the ways we've discussed so far (and any more you can devise) and use it often.

Salting the List

Notice we've referred to *renting* your lists, not buying them. This is how it's done in the direct-mail world—unless you are swapping or purchasing outright as we described above, you rent a one-time or one-year use of the list from the list broker. You're free to take any names that respond to your mailing and incorporate them into your very own house list (which, of course, you can use anytime you like), but you can't use the entire list more than once unless you rent it again.

How does the list broker or the owner know if you decide to cheat and use the list without renting it again? They salt in bogus names (e.g., their mother, brother, or dog) and addresses; then, if Mom, Bubba, or Fido receives your mailing, you are caught. So don't try it.

The rental fee for most lists runs from $100 to $150 per thousand names. You'll also be charged extra fees for any selects or special qualifiers you might choose. (Instead of going with a broad band of Pacific Northwest restaurateurs, for instance, you might ask for restaurants in the Pacific Northwest with fewer than 25 employees and annual revenues of more than $200,000.)

Brochure (Side One)

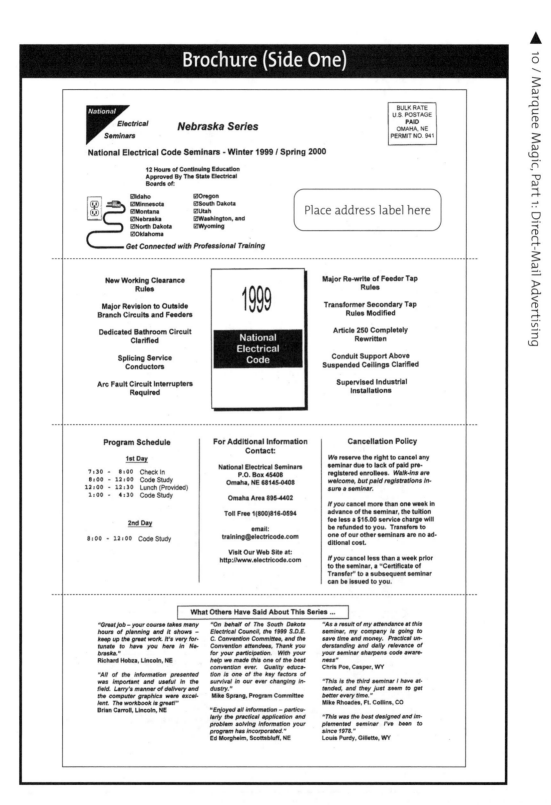

National
Electrical
Seminars

Nebraska Series

National Electrical Code Seminars - Winter 1999 / Spring 2000

12 Hours of Continuing Education
Approved By The State Electrical
Boards of:

☑Idaho ☑Oregon
☑Minnesota ☑South Dakota
☑Montana ☑Utah
☑Nebraska ☑Washington, and
☑North Dakota ☑Wyoming
☑Oklahoma

Get Connected with Professional Training

Place address label here

New Working Clearance
Rules

Major Revision to Outside
Branch Circuits and Feeders

Dedicated Bathroom Circuit
Clarified

Splicing Service
Conductors

Arc Fault Circuit Interrupters
Required

1999

**National
Electrical
Code**

Major Re-write of Feeder Tap
Rules

Transformer Secondary Tap
Rules Modified

Article 250 Completely
Rewritten

Conduit Support Above
Suspended Ceilings Clarified

Supervised Industrial
Installations

Program Schedule

1st Day

7:30 - 8:00   Check In
8:00 - 12:00   Code Study
12:00 - 12:30   Lunch (Provided)
1:00 - 4:30   Code Study

2nd Day

8:00 - 12:00   Code Study

For Additional Information Contact:

National Electrical Seminars
P.O. Box 45408
Omaha, NE 68145-0408

Omaha Area 895-4402

Toll Free 1(800)816-0594

email:
training@electricode.com

Visit Our Web Site at:
http://www.electricode.com

Cancellation Policy

We reserve the right to cancel any seminar due to lack of paid pre-registered enrollees. Walk-ins are welcome, but paid registrations insure a seminar.

If you cancel more than one week in advance of the seminar, the tuition fee less a $15.00 service charge will be refunded to you. Transfers to one of our other seminars are no additional cost.

If you cancel less than a week prior to the seminar, a "Certificate of Transfer" to a subsequent seminar can be issued to you.

What Others Have Said About This Series ...

"Great job – your course takes many hours of planning and it shows – keep up the great work. It's very fortunate to have you here in Nebraska."
Richard Hobza, Lincoln, NE

"All of the information presented was important and useful in the field. Larry's manner of delivery and the computer graphics were excellent. The workbook is great!"
Brian Carroll, Lincoln, NE

"On behalf of The South Dakota Electrical Council, the 1999 S.D.E.C. Convention Committee, and the Convention attendees, Thank you for your participation. With your help we made this one of the best convention ever. Quality education is one of the key factors of survival in our ever changing industry."
Mike Sprang, Program Committee

"Enjoyed all information – particularly the practical application and problem solving information your program has incorporated."
Ed Morgheim, Scottsbluff, NE

"As a result of my attendance at this seminar, my company is going to save time and money. Practical understanding and daily relevance of your seminar sharpens code awareness"
Chris Poe, Casper, WY

"This is the third seminar I have attended, and they just seem to get better every time."
Mike Rhoades, Ft. Collins, CO

"This was the best designed and implemented seminar I've been to since 1978."
Louis Purdy, Gillette, WY

Brochure (Side Two)

Larry is one of the *few full-time professional* National Electrical Code® trainers in the country. More than 20,000 electricians, electrical contractors, and engineers have attended his workshops. Larry's *mastery* of the electrical industry comes from thirty-one years experience as apprentice electrician, journeyman electrician, master electrician, state electrical inspector, fire and accident investigator, draftsman, electrical estimator, project manager, purchasing agent, consultant, speaker, trainer and author.

The hallmark of Larry's seminars is entertaining, interactive, practical electrical code training.

The National Speakers Association recently granted Larry the professional designation of *Certified Speaking Professional* (CSP). He is the only Code® trainer in the United States to be so recognized.

Larry T. Smith, CSP

Grand Island, NE **Aug 20 & 21, 1999** Holiday Inn I-80 & US 261 (308) 384-7770	**Gering, NE** **Oct 22 & 23, 1999** Gering Civic Center 1050 M Street (308) 436-6888	**Columbus, NE** **Feb 4 & 5, 2000** New World Inn Highway 30 & 81 South (800) 433-1492
Lincoln, NE **Sep 24 & 25, 1999** NE Center for Continuing Education 33rd and Holdrege Streets (402) 472-3435	**Lincoln, NE** **Jan 7 & 8, 2000** NE Center for Continuing Education 33rd and Holdrege Streets (402) 472-3435	**Fremont, NE** **Feb 11 & 12, 2000** Bonanza 830 E 23rd Street (402) 721-4422
Omaha, NE **Oct 8 & 9, 1999** Four Point Sheraton 4888 South 118th Street (402) 895-1000	**Omaha, NE** **Jan 21 & 22, 2000** Four Point Sheraton 4888 South 118th Street (402) 895-1000	**Council Bluffs, IA** **Mar 3 & 4, 2000** Best Western I-80/29 & 24th Street Exit (712) 322-3150
Kearney, NE **Oct 15 & 16, 1999** Fort Kearney Inn 80 South 2nd Avenue (800) 652-7245	**Sioux City, IA** **Jan 28 & 29, 2000** Sioux City Convention Center 801 4th Street (712) 279-4800	**Norfolk, NE** **Mar 24 & 25, 2000** Ramada Inn 1227 Omaha Avenue (402) 371-7000

Tuition Fee

You can attend this seminar for $109.00 or *you can register 10 days prior to the seminar and be entitled to a $10.00 discount.*

The tuition fee includes a copy of *Illustrated Changes in the 1999 National Electrical Code and Practical Code Review*, coffee during breaks, certificate of attendance and *you will be our guest for lunch on the first day.*

Accommodations

Lodging arrangements are your responsibility. Most of the hotels are offering special rates. Contact them directly and tell them you will be attending the National Electrical Seminars workshop.

Registration Information

Mail the registration form and tuition fee to:
National Electrical Seminars
P.O. Box 45408
Omaha, NE 68145-0408, *or*

Call us today at:
(402) 895-4402 in the Omaha area, or toll free at 1(800)816-0594 to register, then mail the tuition fee, *or*

Fax the completed registration form to:
(402) 894-1814, then mail the tuition fee, *or*

Visit our web page at *electricode.com*. We invite you to register on-line.
Our Federal Tax ID Number is 47-0767172

✂ --

Please Type or Print All Information

Name _____

Address _____

City-State-Zip _____

Home Telephone (   ) _____

Soc. Sec. No. _____

Company Name _____

Company Address _____

Company Telephone (   ) _____

I will be attending the seminar located in:

_____ on _____

Registration Fee	
Early registration with $10.00 discount	$ 99.00
Registration Fee	$109.00
____ 1999 Code Books @ $38.00 ea.	$_____
Total fee enclosed	$_____

National Electrical Seminars
P.O. Box 45408
Omaha, NE 68145-0408

Self-Mailer

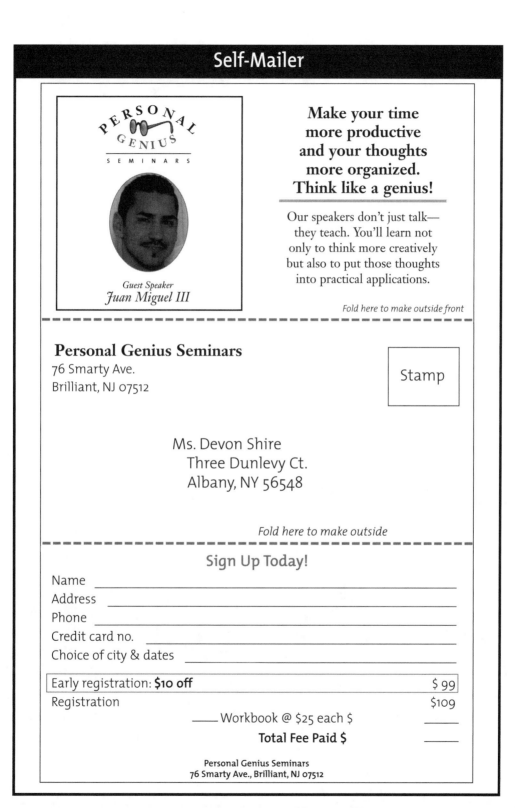

P E R S O N A L

G E N I U S

S E M I N A R S

Guest Speaker
Juan Miguel III

**Make your time
more productive
and your thoughts
more organized.
Think like a genius!**

Our speakers don't just talk—
they teach. You'll learn not
only to think more creatively
but also to put those thoughts
into practical applications.

Fold here to make outside front

Personal Genius Seminars
76 Smarty Ave.
Brilliant, NJ 07512

Stamp

Ms. Devon Shire
Three Dunlevy Ct.
Albany, NY 56548

Fold here to make outside

Sign Up Today!

Name _____

Address _____

Phone _____

Credit card no. _____

Choice of city & dates _____

Early registration: **$10 off**	$ 99
Registration	$109
_____ Workbook @ $25 each $	_____
Total Fee Paid $	_____

Personal Genius Seminars
76 Smarty Ave., Brilliant, NJ 07512

Marquee Magic, Part 2
Promo Kits and Media Time

Although unsolicited brochures or letters can work wonders, they're not the only way to go. Some seminar professionals—particularly those who do private rather than public seminars—never use unsolicited material at all, relying on referrals from past participants, speakers bureaus, and other sundry sources to garner initial interest. Then, when potential clients request information, they swing into promotional mode.

Promo Kits

Gail Hahn of Fun*cilitators, for example, sends promo kits to potential clients. "I send the full kit to prospects who have money and a date and sometimes to those who just have the budget and want to know more than just price-shopping," Hahn says. "I don't send it first thing [at the first inquiry] since it gets costly to mail. I don't send a video unless they ask for it or unless it seems that they need it to make a positive decision.

"If people are just cold-calling and price-shopping," Hahn continues, "I steer them to my web site first. It has a media center page allowing them to hear me live doing radio talk show interviews from several shows—three minutes each—as well as download some of my articles. I ask them if that's enough info or if they need something in hard copy. I try never to fax things since the presentation isn't as attractive—the colors don't come through.

Spread the Word

Sending mail is not the only way to encourage sales. In fact, most seminar professionals will tell you that the absolute best way to spread the word is by word-of-mouth.

"Direct mail gets people to our public seminars," Larry Smith of National Electrical Seminars in Omaha, Nebraska, explains. "Many participants leave our public seminars and then arrange for a private seminar for their companies. The best possible advertising is to have the best possible product; word-of-mouth takes care of the rest."

Gail Hahn agrees. One of her strongest marketing methods, she says, is just being out there, doing sessions and getting leads from the audience. "My session evaluations have a place for recommendations," explains the Reston, Virginia, speaker, "and people always have other associations or friends who belong to other things that need speakers."

Dr. Jerry Old in Shawnee, Kansas, echoes these sentiments. "By far, the greatest advertising is word-of-mouth from satisfied attendees," he says. "Nothing I know works better or is more cost-effective."

"If they're not 'qualified' candidates (no exact date, no money—yet), then I used to send them a contact sheet," says the Reston, Virginia, speaker. "But because my web site has just gone gangbusters, I send them to the web site, which has a lot more information than the contact sheet. Sometimes they want something printed—if they're trying to get a bunch of information from several speakers and have to lay it all out on the table in front of a group, then I'll send them the sheet. But I try to steer them to my web site because it has everything on it. And it's cost-effective because those kits are about $10 with the color copies, heavy-duty stationery, custom-made folders, and videos."

Bright Idea

Use your imagination with promotional materials. Besides postcards, how about sending bookmarks embellished with your company name and logo (use your desktop-publishing program), greeting cards to commemorate different events (not only the usual holidays but different ones like National Pickle Week for people in the food industry or Thomas Edison's birthday) to illustrate that you're full of bright ideas.

Gail's contact sheet—in keeping with all her other promotional materials—reflects the learn-to-have-fun nature of her programs. "It's glossy and has purple writing," she explains, "with a cutout photo of me on the front and a cartoon of me on the back. I also use those sheets for prospecting since they're a quick overview and easy to read. It's one of the first pieces of propaganda, er, promotional material they will receive. I always send a cover letter or press release along with the contact sheet."

Dr. Jerry Old in Shawnee, Kansas, has his own take on the promo kit. "I have a one-page color flier with my picture and a description of my seminar or program," he says. "It includes references and a few comments (positive ones!) from former clients. It's not glossy but is on high-resolution paper as that seemed most cost-effective since I'm just starting in the business. I mail it flat (not folded) with a copy of my videotape to any organization or individual who expresses an interest."

Assembling Your Kit

If you plan to offer private seminars, you'll want a promo (for promotional) or presentation kit. Here are the elements you'll want to include:

- cover letter
- business card
- flier (also called a *content sheet*, *contact sheet*, or *one-sheet*) describing your program
- fee schedule
- client list
- testimonials and letters of recommendation

▲

Robo-Marketing

Acompany web site can act as your robotic (or maybe clone) marketing person, offering promotional materials to potential clients 24 hours a day, seven days a week. And you don't have to be anywhere near the office!

"The web site has been a tremendous boost to my marketing," Gail Hahn of Reston, Virginia-based Fun*Cilitators says, "since I can steer prospects there while I'm on the road and not able to send out packets. It also serves them well since they can get the info immediately and also let others on their conference committees view the page from wherever they happen to be—many committees for associations are located in different states."

Denise Dudley of Mission, Kansas-based SkillPath agrees. "We have a web site you can visit and explore and then register from," she says. "The direct mail leads people to the web site to check out other programs."

Hahn gets lots of unsolicited business from her web site. "It's just huge," she says. "Yesterday four people called; I've got six contracts to type up."

To what does she attribute her site's success? She has 15 domain names that reflect her company's focus, such as www.funatwork.net, all of which direct web surfers to her company's main site, www.funcilitators.com. "I've reserved names of books that I'm going to publish and other key words that people use to look for [the type of programs I do]," Gail explains. "I think a lot of people find me through that. I'm also linked to a lot of other sites that are portals for speakers, like speakers direct.com, speaker.com, speaking.com, speakersplatform.com, humoru.com, experts.com, and nsaspeaker.org. Some of those drive people to my site."

Hahn doesn't do any costly internet advertising like pay-per-click. Instead she puts key words in meta-tags (concise web site descriptions that are picked up by search engines) and also—low-tech but effective—is careful to feature her web site address on all her printed materials, including her letterhead.

- articles or newsletters by you
- articles about you
- black-and-white photos of you
- postcards
- "toys" or other goodies
- promotional treats like coffee and creamer packets, candies, or whatever else you can dream up

Use the checklist on page 176 to make sure you don't forget anything.

Anatomy of a Promo Kit

Now that you've got the overview, let's look at these elements one by one:

- *Cover letter.* This is a letter to your prospective client that officially introduces you, explains what you can do for her company and why you're the best one for the job, and invites a reply. Take a look at the sample on page 177 for an idea of what to say and how to say it.

- *Business card.* Even though your name, phone number, and other contact information are on your letterhead, you should always include a business card as well. It shows that you're a professional and also gives that prospect a ready reference that she can pin on her bulletin board, tape to her computer monitor, place in her card file, or paste on her forehead.

- *Flier, content, or contact sheet.* This is your program in a nutshell—a one-page description of the seminar or workshop that (remember!) stresses the benefits. The content sheet should give the high points you'll cover (a teaser just like in

Bright Idea

Use your imagination! If your niche is show horses, can you supply ribbons for show winners? If it's gardening, can you sponsor a yard beautification program? Whatever you can do to get your name in front of the public in a favorable way will add to your image—and your income.

Clueless

You'll often get prospects who don't have a clue as to what they want in a program, says seminar professional Denise Dudley. They've decided on a retreat for their salespeople or a keynote speech for their annual conference, but as far as a subject, it's a complete blank. In that case, you can send them the works—everything including the kitchen sink—or you can help them narrow down the choices.

Dudley suggests talking with them on the phone to determine if, for instance, they want a serious work session or if (like girls) they basically just wanna have fun. An association of accountants might need eight continuing education units (otherwise known as CEUs) for which you might suggest hard-core management skills or a more lighthearted communications skills session. Then you tell them "Here's what I think you need." And they're delighted to have you make the decision for them.

your direct-mail brochure), a smattering of testimonials, a brief bio explaining why you are (or your presenter is) the best person to deliver the program, and a photo of you. Make sure you put your contact info (phone number, e-mail address, etc.) on the page, too, so no one can possibly lose track of how to reach you. Check out the sample on page 178.

Bright Idea

Corporate and private clients can sometimes decide in the 11th hour that they just have to have a presenter tomorrow. Pitching yourself as a reliable pinch hitter is a good way to gain gigs.

- *Fee schedule.* This is just what it says: your menu of prices for your programs, as well as for any extra-income goodies you may have. Take a look at the sample on page 179. Be sure to note the "Investment" section at the bottom of the page. This is important stuff—tailor yours to your company but don't leave it out.

Not Always!

Traditional print ads in newspapers and magazines usually don't pull as well as direct mail for the seminar professional—but not always! "Newspaper ads worked fairly well for me," Dr. Jerry Old says of the advertising he did when he started his seminar business, "for the age and type of people I was targeting—older or 'Vintage People.' They seem to get more of their information from reading than a younger market might.

"The ads were generally a standard two columns wide or about 4 inches by 3 inches," the Shawnee, Kansas, speaker explains. "We ran ads starting 21 days before the event, twice the first week, three times the second week, and four times the third week, depending on prices. Most newspapers give you a better deal the more often it's repeated, and some will throw in a free run after six times.

"The content included the title, my picture, the place, time, and how to obtain tickets, and a short sentence—four to five words only—about the seminar. I don't feel people will read long or busy ads, so we kept them very short."

Since moving from a small town to the big city two years ago, Dr. Old hasn't done any newspaper advertising. "We haven't found the need or maybe the time," he says. "It worked pretty well in the community where we were because we were pretty well known. Here, I'm not sure an ad would work; people might just say, 'Who?'"

- *Client list.* This, too, is just what it says it is—a list of your satisfied clients. If you're just starting out and you don't have any clients to list, leave this out. It's OK—you'll still have your testimonials to recommend you.

- *Testimonials and letters of recommendation.* It's always a good idea to put a pageful in your promo kit. This assures the prospect that she's making the right choice because other professional people have been delighted with your programs. Use letters of recommendation if you've got 'em—they're another form of testimonial. It's perfectly acceptable to ask those satisfied clients to write them for you to put into your kit.

 Beware!
Promotional pieces that look stunning in living color often look muddy, blurry or even illegible when faxed. If prospects need information in a major hurry, use FedEx to send your package, make up a special black-and-white faxable content sheet that will serve until they receive your "real" kit in the mail, or develop an e-mail kit.

"I send testimonial letters that go with the prospect's industry," Gail Hahn says. "I'll give them probably six or eight clients who have been, for instance, in the banking industry, which means more to them than letters from a truckers association would. They know that I know a little bit about their business, their challenges, and the needs of their industry."

- *Articles or newsletters by you or your presenter.* This doesn't mean a two-inch sheaf made up of everything you've ever written. But it does mean that you can and should provide reprints of articles written on the topics the client has asked about as well as a sample of your company newsletter, if you have one.

- *Articles about you or your presenter.* These are magazine and newspaper articles written about you and your company that pertain to the topic the client is interested in. If the client has asked about team-building seminars, don't send articles that tout you as a professional organizer—it confuses the issue and makes it seem as though you don't have team-building experience.

- *Black-and-white photos.* People want to see who and what they're paying for. So put in a few photos (on one page) of you to lay to rest worries that you might be too decrepit, too inexperienced or just cheesy. Wear your professional presenter duds, be they a suit and tie or your fairy godmother frock, and try for at least two shots: a head shot with you smiling into the camera and one or two showing you in action as a presenter.

- *Postcard.* This is an optional item, not a must-have. If you've already made up a batch of postcards to use as stand-alone promo items, as Gail Hahn has done (see "Style Networking" on page 172, then go ahead and add one into your kit. If not, don't worry about it.

Let's Talk

When prospective clients call Nance Cheifetz to ask about her team-building and employee recognition programs, she interviews them before sending out a promo kit. "Before I send you a package, let's sit and talk about what you're really looking for," Cheifetz tells prospects.

"It's a very different [approach]," explains the owner of Novato, California's Sense of Delight. "A lot of people say, 'Here are my six programs' or 'Download my programs off my web site.' My biggest strength is my ability to be creative and customize things. If I can get somebody on the phone who's really interested and actually has a budget, then I will find out what they need. Then they'll say, 'Send me a proposal.' Asking all these questions makes a huge difference."

Here are the kinds of questions Cheifetz asks:

○ What are your goals for the session?
○ What's the mix of participants?
○ What's the age range?
○ What's the gender mix?
○ What would be a success for you?
○ How much time will we have?
○ Are we dealing with introverts or extroverts?
○ Will participants be sitting in a meeting all day or all week?
○ Will participants be having liquor at lunch?

- *Folder.* This is the first thing in the kit your prospect will see, so make it look good. It should carry the theme of all your printed pieces, with the same colors, fonts, and graphic design elements, and should say who and what your company is and does right upfront. Use the type of folder that has pockets on both inside covers, into which you can stuff your printed materials.

- *Audio and/or video demo.* You know all about these, so send them. Like Hahn, you may want to exercise some discretion about how serious your prospect is before you pop them into your package, but do make them a consideration.

- *Back-of-the-room (BOR) products.* Because hardcover books and videotapes can get expensive to mail, this is another area where you may want to send them only to prospects who are more serious, or who you're more seriously interested in impressing. It's not necessary to send every product in your inventory, but if you've got something impressive and/or splashy that you feel will make the difference between a sale and a pass, by all means add it to your promo kit package.

- *Promotional treats.* You may want to add some special attention-grabber—cookies, chocolates, confetti, or even something that doesn't begin with the letter "C."

Nance Cheifetz of Northern California's Sense of Delight, who bills herself as a Corporate Fairy Godmother, used to add goodies to match her theme. "I sent fairy dust and cookies, and I mailed it in an unusual tube so I knew the package would be opened immediately." After the anthrax scare, however, Cheifetz realized that sending "dust" through the mail was no longer an option. "But I still send toys or something fun to everyone," she says.

Gail Hahn tucks a gourmet chocolate bar into her kits. "It has a customized wrapper that says 'You're FUNominal' and then it has all the ingredients to make a FUNominal person, like a jigger of joy and pinch of playful professionalism," she explains. "I put that in along with their panic buttons and fun meters [two of Hahn's BOR products]. A lot of times that helps push them over the edge of me against the competition because they can buy that stuff for all their attendees, and they love that." And who can resist chocolate?

Bright Idea

As long as your topics are light, don't be afraid to have a little fun with your testimonials (as well as with your kit as a whole). Seminar entrepreneur Gail Hahn has one that reads, "She's always loved to talk and have fun. She's perfect for this!—Phoenix, AZ (OK, that one was from my parents)."

Value-Added Advertising

While you've got that let's-advertise thinking cap on, consider what else you can do that will not only keep your name before your public but add value to your advertising and income. Gail Hahn sends an annual or semi-annual e-zine to clients and prospects. Subscriptions are free ("I know you have to give to get," Hahn says).

By doing this, the Reston, Virginia, speaker accomplishes three things:

1. keeps her name upfront so clients remember her
2. maintains her image as an expert
3. gets names for her mailing list from participants' business cards

Use your imagination and have fun—just make sure that whatever it is fits in with the topics and ambience you're selling. And don't feel that you must put a treat into your kit—this is a totally optional item.

Free Advertising

Yes! While, in the words of the old cliché, there's no such thing as a free lunch, there are some terrific things you can do to get free advertising. Of course, you have to put forth effort, intelligence, and creativity, so it's not free as in "you don't have to lift a finger," but that's OK. The rewards are worth it.

Smart Tip

"For all seminars—public or private—I respond with a written confirmation to whoever is in charge," says seminar professional Dr. Jerry Old, "repeating the date, time, title, fee, etc. Neither my clients nor I like any surprises. I have found that occasionally expectations may be different from what I have in mind, and I like to find that out early."

Style Networking

Consider augmenting your direct-mail advertising and promo kits with additional mailings—to current as well as prospective clients.

"I hardly send any prospecting letters/contact sheets out," says Gail Hahn of Reston, Virginia's Fun*cilitators. "That's just not my style." Hahn used to send quarterly newsletters and some postcards in between with a handwritten note (the effective Chinese water torture method, as she calls it). "Postcards are quick and easy and get your attention without having to be opened, and with an attention-grabbing photo, they really work," she says.

But that's not all Hahn did to insure that her materials were read. "I also had my newsletter folded in a larger scale and strange shape to grab attention in the pile of mail in the box," she says. "I also put something different printed above their name to encourage them to open it." Like what? She used a fun font that says "A Live Wire for the Awesome: (fill in name and address)" or she sprinkled a few colorful star-shaped stickers above the address—both of which made that piece enticing to open.

Now that her company, which just celebrated its seventh birthday, needs less hard-core promotion, Hahn has replaced the quarterly newsletter and postcards with annual or semi-annual postcard mailings, and an annual or semi-annual e-zine, which is much more cost- and time-effective.

Bonus Marketing Department

Speakers bureaus can be excellent advertising and promotion venues—if you use them properly. "The bureau is another marketing department," Gail Hahn says. "It's another person out there selling you." The Reston, Virginia, fun facilitator believes what she says; she's currently registered with 30 bureaus.

Like any other avenue, however, you have to put in some effort to make speakers bureaus work for you. With hundreds or even thousands of speakers on file at each bureau, you can easily get lost in the shuffle. It's up to you to keep your name in the forefront of the bunch. Hahn makes sure her bureaus get any postcards or press releases she sends out. She also sends copies of any new testimonials she receives. This reminds the bureaus she's out there and available and also helps them market her by providing credibility-type material.

The Magazine Expert

So what are these free advertising opportunities? One, as you know, is word-of-mouth. Another—as we promised to divulge at the top of the chapter—is print media. Take advantage of the thousands of magazines and journals out there by writing articles for publication.

That's what Gail Hahn does. "People won't look at ads," she says, "but they will read articles." Your credibility as an expert soars—if you're in a magazine, you must be a pro, people reason—and as your credibility takes wing, so does your desirability as a speaker. And the benefits don't stop with the reader. People won't tear out an ad, but they'll tear out an article and pass it along to friends and relatives, so you get the word-of-mouth effect even in print.

Medicine or Waste Management?

What publications should you submit to? Take a look at your target audience; then go for the trade or professional journals they read,

Smart Tip

Tip...

Tailor your promo kit to the prospective client's request. If an employee training manager calls and asks for a program on team-building, for instance, your package—including cover letter, content sheet, and testimonials—should describe only your team-building seminar and not your other programs.

whether it's the *Journal of the American Medical Association* or *Waste Management Professional*. If you're going for a general audience, you can also target general interest publications—the ones you find in the supermarket checkout lines (not *The National Enquirer*, but things like *Woman's Day* or *Self*). General interest magazines are much more difficult to get into than trade and professional publications, but if your topic and your writing skills are terrific—and if the editor's in the right frame of mind—you can do it.

The best way to approach the issue is to head down to your local public library and sit down with the latest copy of *Writer's Market* (you can't check it out, so bring change for copying pages) or pick up a copy at a bookstore. Thumb through this hefty volume—you'll be amazed at the number of publications in every imaginable specialty—and pick out the ones that might be good targets for your articles.

Back at home, call the magazine or journal to find out which editor to send your piece to; then ask to speak to him briefly and find out if he'd be interested. Keep your conversation short and professional—editors are busy people.

When you elicit interest, send a one-page query letter—written as temptingly as your direct-mail brochure or promo kit content sheet—describing the article you plan to write and asking the editor to contact you if he's interested.

If the editor is interested, you write the article—and there's your free advertising. And as bonus, you'll get paid. So not only is the advertising free, but they're paying you for the privilege. Pretty cool, eh?

You can also write articles for the inhouse publications of client corporations and associations. You get paid and you also keep your name upfront where they'll remember you and call on you for additional seminars.

Public Relations

In any business, public relations is an important aspect to consider. Good public relations can accomplish two things:

1. put your company name out to people who may not have heard of you
2. keep people who are already your customers thinking fondly of you and thus repeat-enrolling

In other words, PR is another terrific source of free advertising. There are all sorts of low-cost techniques you can use. Try some of the following:

> **Bright Idea**
>
> Can't afford that newspaper or radio advertising? Offer to barter—"free" advertising in exchange for giving a customer service or other seminar to the newspaper or radio station's staff.

- Local groups are always looking for guest speakers. Offer yourself on a free, or *pro bono*, basis to local associations or clubs that match your target audience. If you're selling motivational seminars, for instance, you can talk to men's clubs, women's groups, business groups from the Jaycees to the Chamber of Commerce to various networking clubs, and even kids' clubs. Just be sure to tailor your topic to your particular audience. Remember that word-of-mouth is a powerful advertising tool and get creative!

- Join any organizations that match your target audience and volunteer for things that will get you and your company recognized—and thought well of. Most people respect volunteers within an organization and consider them experts in the organization's area of interest, which heightens your credibility.

- How about going live on the air? Volunteer yourself for a local radio station's chat show. You can discuss your niche—for instance, health care, business travel, or romance writing. Listeners can call in with questions. When they talk to you—on the air!—they'll be interested in enrolling in your seminars. And remember word-of-mouth. They'll tell their friends and relatives.

- Offer free enrollment in your seminar or pricier (therefore splashier) BOR products as prizes for charity events.

Promo Kit Checklist

Here's a list of the elements you'll want to include in your promo or presentation kit.

❑ Cover letter

❑ Business card

❑ Flier, content, or contact sheet

❑ Fee schedule

❑ Client list

❑ Testimonials and letters of recommendation

❑ Articles or newsletters by me or my presenter(s)

❑ Articles about me or my presenter(s)

❑ Black-and-white photos of me or my presenter(s)

❑ Postcards

❑ Folder to put all this stuff in

❑ Audio and/or video demo

❑ BOR products (listed below):

_____

_____

_____

_____

_____

❑ Promotional treats (listed below):

_____

_____

_____

_____

_____

Introductory Cover Letter

So Romantic Seminars
Empowering Romance Writers for Success

September 10, 200x

Ms. Summer Strand
Silver Bay Writers Group
1432 Moonbeam Lane
Silver Bay, FL 30000

Dear Ms. Strand:

I enjoyed talking with you this morning! It sounds like you've got a fascinating, professional group of writers. So Romantic can fulfill a variety of functions at your Winter Conference, providing everything from the awards banquet keynote speech to half-day workshops featuring hands-on participation to lively one-hour seminars.

I've enclosed a content sheet that describes our most popular conference program, a fee schedule, a listing of some of the groups we've worked with, and a short video sampler of our seminars, along with a bouquet of other So Romantic materials.

Our goal is not just to speak but to empower—to help every writer become a success. We've guided many romance novelists from budding novice to published star in full flower, as well as helped those already in bloom to keep from fading on the vine. I'm confident that we can make a positive contribution to your conference. I'll call you within the next week to answer any questions and discuss how we can meet your needs. We look forward to working with you!

Very best,

Natalie Norman
Natalie Norman,
CEF (Chief Empowerment Facilitator)

630 Rose Lane, Honeysuckle, CA 94444 (000) 000-2311
e-mail: natalie@soromanticseminars.com
www.soromanticseminars.com

Contact Sheet

So Romantic Seminars
Empowering Romance Writers for Success

"Making a Splash: Attracting that Editor's Attention"

Every writer knows penning that wonderful story is only half the battle. The other half is getting the editor to pick it up and read it—and then, of course, to buy it. In this lively, empowering program, Natalie shares the secrets of making a splash with editors. Learn how to:

○ create simple promotional tools that will get that manuscript opened and read
○ develop a rapport with the editor
○ create new writing opportunities from the manuscript already on the editor's desk

An award-winning romance novelist and editor herself, Natalie knows what it's like on both sides of the desk. In this unique half-day program, she shares her insights and tips in a lively, hands-on fashion that gives each participant the tools to make his or her own splash.

After attending your "Making A Splash" workshop, I sold my first novel to Moonglow Books and signed a contract for three more. Thank you, Natalie! I couldn't have done it without you!
—Kelly Spring, Catewood, MD

Your workshop was filled with so many wonderful tips and ideas— I can't think when I've come away from a seminar more inspired. Thank you from the bottom of my romantic heart.
—T.J. Sido, Provence, LA

Our conference was a great success thanks to So Romantic. We look forward to using your seminars and workshops again next year.
—Angie Barron, Crown City Writers Guild, Tiara, WA

630 Rose Lane, Honeysuckle, CA 94444 (000) 000-2311
e-mail: natalie@soromanticseminars.com
www.soromanticseminars.com

Fee Schedule

So Romantic Seminars
Empowering Romance Writers for Success

Programs & Perks

○ Keynote speech (up to one hour) — $2,000
○ Half-day session (up to 3 hours) — 2,500
○ Full-day session (up to 6 hours) — 3,000
○ Each additional one-hour session per date — 500
○ Consulting/coaching — 100/hr.
○ Article for client publication — TBA*

Books

From Bud to Bloom: Successful Manuscript Sales — $15
(save $5)
Coffee & Chocolate: Creative Tips for Writers — $12
(save $3.95)

Tapes

"From Bud to Bloom: Successful Manuscript Sales" — $20
    4 audiotapes (save $5)
"Coffee & Chocolate: Creative Tips for Writers" — $12
    2 audiotapes (save $3.95)

Other Perks

You Can Do It! Coffee Mug — $7
Indispensable encouragement and cheer for every writer's desk
Writer's Tips Daily Calendar — $12
Another must-have for every writer's desk, featuring daily doses of tips and inspiration from Natalie Norman

Investment

Client is responsible for all professional services plus expenses including travel, lodging, meals, taxes, shipping, and educational materials. A 50 percent deposit is due within 14 days of booking, with the balance due on or before the date of service. Quotes are valid for 90 days from quotation date. We guarantee 100 percent satisfaction or your investment will be refunded. (We have never been asked to do this!)

630 Rose Lane, Honeysuckle, CA 94444 (000) 000-2311
e-mail: natalie@soromanticseminars.com
www.soromanticseminars.com

Note: TBA means "to be arranged." You might aim for something like $300 per article.

12

The Check's in the Mail

Effectively Controlling Your Finances

Whether you're a chronic number cruncher or one of the finance-phobic, you will want to give your company periodic financial checkups. "Why?" you ask. "I already did all that math stuff in the start-up chapter." Yup. That was the prenatal exam for the precious baby that's your business. When you've gone through the birthing process and that precocious tot is toddling around, you will want periodic checks to make sure your offspring is as healthy as you think it is.

If there is a problem, you will find out before it becomes critical. For instance, if you discover that your income barely covers your printing or operating expenses, you can change gears along with the number of direct-mail pieces you send out.

Financial checkups don't have to be negative.

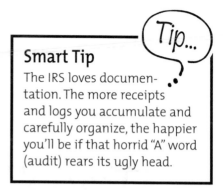

Smart Tip

The IRS loves documentation. The more receipts and logs you accumulate and carefully organize, the happier you'll be if that horrid "A" word (audit) rears its ugly head.

They can give you a rosy glow by demonstrating how well you're doing—possibly even better than you expected. If you've been saving for a new printer or software upgrade, or if you're hoping to take on an employee, you can judge how close you are to achieving that goal.

Making a Statement

An *income statement*, also called a *profit-and-loss statement*, charts the revenues and operating costs of your business over a specific period of time, usually a month. Check out the sample income statements on pages 185 and 186 for our two hypothetical seminar companies, TravelTeach Seminars and So Romantic Seminars. TravelTeach, a homebased newbie with no employees except its owner, so far has a net profit of $20,000.

So Romantic, with three years of business under its bodice, makes its base in an industrial park near the airport, employs a secretary and an assistant in addition to the owner, and tabulates annual net profits of $200,000. Neither owner draws a salary; they both rely on a percentage of the net profit for their income.

You'll want to tailor your income statement to your particular business. To make the statement really right, you'll need to prorate items that are paid annually, such as business licenses and tax-time accounting fees and pop those figures into your monthly statement. For example, if you pay annual insurance premiums of $600, divide this figure by 12 and add the resulting $50 to your insurance expense.

Use the monthly income statement worksheet on page 187 to chart your own income statement. You'll be surprised at how much fun finances can be!

Taxing Matters

When you earn money from your wisely planned and brilliantly delivered seminars, someone will be queuing up for a piece of the action: Uncle Sam. If your budget allows, you should also engage an accountant. You probably won't need him or her for your daily or monthly concerns, but it's well worth the expense to have someone in the know at the reins when April 15 rolls around, or for those rare but "panicsville" questions that come up now and again.

Your tax deductions should be about the same as those for any other small or home-based business. You can deduct a percentage of your home office so long as you're using it solely as an office. These deductions include all normal office expenses plus interest, taxes, insurance, and depreciation (this is where the accountant comes in handy). The IRS has added in all sorts of permutations such as that the total amount of the deduction is limited by the gross income you derive from the business activity minus all your other business expenses apart from those related to the home office. And you thought that new board game you got for Christmas had complicated rules!

Basically, the IRS doesn't want you to come up with so many home office deductions that you end up paying no tax at all. If, after reading all the lowdown, you are still confused, consult with your accountant.

You can also call the IRS with questions at convenient 800 numbers all over the country. You may have to go through voice-mail hell and the hold period forever, but once you get a live being on the line, the IRS is surprisingly friendly.

Driving Miss Seminar Professional

What else can you deduct? Business-related phone calls, the cost of business equipment and supplies (again, so long as you're truly using them solely for your business), subscriptions to professional and trade journals, and auto expenses. These accrue when you drive your trusty vehicle in the course of doing business or seeking business.

Wheel and Deal

As a seminar professional, you need to keep your costs pared to the bone to make a profit. So whether you're inquiring about print advertising space, printing or letter shop services, copywriting, graphics, or vendors' products, the key word is negotiate. Don't accept the first price anybody quotes you. Ask for a better deal and, surprisingly enough, you'll often get it.

Besides bargaining, shop around. Get quotes from several printers or list brokers. Evaluate not only price but factors like time estimated to complete a project and company qualifications. Don't be afraid to ask questions. Nobody expects you to be an expert on everything, especially not immediately. If you don't ask, you don't learn.

In other words, you're chalking up deductible mileage every time you motor out to give a seminar, visit vendors', printers' or videographers' offices, or take a spin upstate to check out meeting sites.

It's wise to keep a log of your business miles. You can buy one of several varieties at your local office supply or stationers, or you can make one yourself. Keep track as you go. It's no fun to have to backtrack at tax time and guesstimate how many miles you drove to how many clients how many times during the year.

Let Me Entertain You

Entertainment expenses, such as wining and dining a client during the course of a meeting or hosting potential customers at a coffee hour, are 50 percent deductible. Keep a log of all these expenses as well, especially if they come to less than $75 a pop, and if you're entertaining at home, have your clients or customers sign a guest book.

Planes, Trains, and Automobiles

When you travel for business purposes, you can deduct airfare, train tickets, rental car mileage, and the like. You can also deduct hotels and meals. And you can even—under certain circumstances—deduct recreational side trips you take with your family while you're traveling on business. Since the IRS allows deductions for any such trip you take to expand your awareness and expertise in your field of business, it makes sense to also take advantage of any conferences or seminars that you can attend—a businessman's holiday to keep abreast of events in your target market or to see how the competition's doing.

TravelTeach Seminars Income Statement

For the month of July 200x		
Monthly Income		
Ticket sales	$1,667	
Product sales	250	
Gross Monthly Income:		$1,917
Monthly Expenses		
Rent	0	
Phone/utilities	75	
Electronic card processing	20	
Employee payroll	0	
Postage	20	
Licenses	8	
Legal services	30	
Accounting services	25	
Office supplies	10	
Shipping supplies	0	
Insurance	90	
Subscriptions/dues	37	
Web hosting	30	
Internet service provider	22	
Loan repayment	0	
Miscellaneous	25	
Total Monthly Expenses		392
Net Monthly Profit		**$1,525**

So Romantic Seminars Income Statement

For the month of July 200x		
Monthly Income		
Ticket sales	$14,500	
Product sales	2,175	
Gross Monthly Income:		$16,675
Monthly Expenses		
Rent	$1,200	
Phone/utilities	1,175	
Electronic card processing	45	
Employee payroll	2,000	
Postage	500	
Licenses	20	
Legal services	100	
Accounting services	100	
Office supplies	50	
Shipping supplies	500	
Insurance	90	
Subscriptions/dues	57	
Web hosting	85	
Internet service provider	50	
Loan repayment	200	
Miscellaneous	50	
Total Monthly Expenses		6,222
Net Monthly Profit		**$10,453**

Monthly Income Statement Worksheet

For the month of:		
Monthly Income		
Gross sales		
Cost of sales		
Gross Monthly Income		
Monthly Expenses		
Rent		
Phone/utilities		
Electronic card processing		
Employee payroll		
Postage		
Licenses		
Legal services		
Accounting services		
Office supplies		
Shipping supplies		
Insurance		
Subscriptions/dues		
Web hosting		
Internet service provider		
Loan repayment		
Miscellaneous		
Total Monthly Expenses		
Net Monthly Profit		

Packed House
or Empty Seats

Most people succeed in the seminar business by following the tried-and-true business methods of persistence and plain old-fashioned hard work with a healthy dose of optimism liberally sprinkled throughout. If we've illustrated anything in this book, we hope it is that becoming a successful seminar professional involves a lot of work. Rewarding and sometimes exhilarating work, but darn hard work nonetheless.

We also hope we've managed to convey that becoming a seminar professional is not the same as becoming an overnight success. It takes lots of market research, loads of planning, and the abundant application of creativity to achieve those repeat clients and customers.

Grind, Sand, and Polish

When the seminar professionals interviewed for this book were asked for some words of advice for beginners, they gave—not surprisingly—some very thoughtful responses.

"Our only product is training," Larry Smith of National Electrical Seminars in Omaha, Nebraska, advises. "The product can and will sell itself only if it is presented at the highest possible level. Be prepared to grind, sand, and polish until it glistens. The harvest can be bountiful, but it comes at a cost, as all worthwhile things do. If the product isn't outstanding, forget about the business. It begins with preparation.

"Preparation is everything," Smith continues. "Prepare for presentations like no one else you have ever seen. The only difference between good and excellent is attention to detail. Your effort will be apparent to the participants, and they will appreciate it.

"It would be so great if all I had to do was work on the presentation," he adds, "but there is always a business demanding attention. Balancing presentation preparation with business management can be overwhelming. It takes a good computer and the rest of the technology that goes with it. Time management is critical; preparation for a presentation must always have first priority."

No Job Beneath You

Denise Dudley of Mission, Kansas-based SkillPath Seminars agrees wholeheartedly with Larry's work ethic. "To make a success," she says, "you have to decide to work very hard." When she and her husband, Jerry, started their business, she adds, no job was beneath them. "Be prepared to answer the phone and take enrollment," she says. "Do everything."

And that includes not striving for glamour right off the bat. You can't build a strong business if you're more concerned about your office ambience—which your clients will never see—than your product. As an example, Dudley explains, her fledgling company bought inexpensive used room partitions that seemed to fall over every hour—but they didn't let it bother them. Instead, they concentrated on creating perfect products, vowing never to let a brochure go out that contained a typo, and to develop the perfect trainers.

Dr. Jerry Old also advises hard work and high standards. "Speak anywhere you can," he says, "even if it has to be for free. You never know who may hear you or who may tell their friends who have a friend who is looking for a speaker! Listen to the audience—they'll tell you what they want to hear and they'll tell you how well you are presenting it.

"Attend workshops about speaking and seminars," the Shawnee, Kansas, doctor adds. "There are some very good ones. Read and continue to learn. Listen to as many great speakers as you can. Listen to tapes. Use humor generously—you have to have an audience's attention before you can be effective. Be professional—have demo tapes and fliers available. Never talk down to the audience—they can tell whether or not you respect them. Be prepared and eventually your time will come."

The Journey

Gail Hahn of Fun*cilitators in Reston, Virginia, advocates starting your new career with a sense of purpose. "Make certain that your passion, purpose, and program are authentic to you and your values," she says, "since you will be living it along your journey of continuous improvement. Enjoy your journey, have fun and play as hard as you work."

Yin and Yang

If you're the type of person who can handle the ups and downs of entrepreneurship in general and the yin and yang of creativity and number-crunching that makes up the seminar professional's world, you'll probably thrive. If not, you may discover during your company's first year of life, or beyond, that the business isn't for you. You may feel that instead of a packed house, you're experiencing empty seats—or an empty heart.

Whether or not you're earning money, the success of your business is contingent on a happiness factor. Because it's a lot of work and a lot of responsibility, you may discover that you'd be just as happy—or even more so—working for someone else. And that's OK. With everything you'll have learned, you'll certainly be a great job candidate.

None of the people interviewed for this book, from a newbie to a veteran with ten years' experience, seems to have any intention of packing it in. Rather, they seem to have a sense of delight at doing what they enjoy, helping others with the same interests, and being a part of the larger world.

Changing Lives

"I feel rewarded that this is a product that's changed people's lives," Dudley says. "We do almost 3,000 seminars a month. I know that we're changing several thousand people's lives. Whether it's tools like using the internet or feeling better about themselves, we're making a difference for people."

But is it all sunshine and roses? Surely, we hear you asking, even the most successful seminar professionals hit some bumps on the road to achievement. So we asked our interviewees about their worst—and best—experiences in the business.

Dudley admits to two worsts, the first being speed reading. "It was the worst topic we ever introduced," she says. Although she and her husband/partner, Jerry, had felt that it was a seminar natural, they came rapidly to the conclusion that it was anything but. And being true pros, they didn't let a miscalculation steam-roll them, but instead let it go and went on. "It died," Dudley says, "a quick but merciful death."

The pair's other worst was something entirely beyond their control—the Gulf War. "It was the first truly televised war," Dudley says, "and when it hit, our phones went totally dead." Why? Everybody was glued to the TV set. "And you can't do dead when you've got seminars," the former psychologist explains. "After you've spent the money for advertising, the best you can do is recover your $300 by canceling the trainer. Otherwise you can never recover the money. We had several bad months."

Along with double "worsts," Dudley also admits to two best experiences: changing customers' and clients' lives for the better through her company's seminars, and positively affecting her employees' lives. "We have an unbelievably diverse population of employees," she says. "I'm so proud of that. We created a work force that works well together. We created a world that's [our company]."

Larry Smith counts his best experience as a routine work occurrence, too. "The best experience in the business," he advises, "is being totally independent, which is something you get to experience every day."

His worst? "Either losing a client," he says, "or spending a day telemarketing."

Ask First

Dr. Jerry Old's worst experience was something else entirely. "I was asked to talk to a company-sponsored group of 200 people," he relates. "It was billed as a motivational workshop for families, including young children. The facility, however, turned out to be two large rooms in an 'L' shape, with a narrow doorway connecting the two halves. The sound system was good in both rooms, but I had to stand in the doorway to speak. When talking to one room, I could not be seen from the other and vice versa.

"To make matters worse," the "Vintage People" expert says, "this doorway was the only way in or out of either room. There was a lot of traffic and kids going in and out. The distractions were great, but I just forged ahead and did the best I could. I got several good comments at the end, but didn't feel too effective. I have learned to ask about the facilities where I'll be speaking!"

Edge of Their Seats

Like his worst, Dr. Old's best experience was something of a surprise. "This is what every speaker lives for," he says. "A group that I spoke to after a nice banquet was reacting to my jokes and message and giving me positive feedback. To close, I told a somewhat inspiring and emotional story about a patient of mine who had accomplished a great deal in spite of a glaring handicap. It got so quiet it almost scared me!

"At the end I looked out over the audience and actually saw at least ten people literally sitting on the edge of their folding chairs," the doctor continues. "I was almost afraid someone was going to fall off. I ended the speech and went to sit down. There was dead silence for what seemed like an eternity. I began to wonder if I had totally failed. Then there was some weak applause that rapidly turned into a crescendo and ended with a standing ovation. It doesn't get any better than that!"

Flying Solo

Gail Hahn counts the occasional fear in flying solo as her worst experience as a seminar professional. "As a solo entrepreneur," she explains, "it's both exciting and scary putting yourself on the edge for a cause rather than just a job. Although your potential is limitless, it's still rattling to have empty space on your speaking schedule. The alternative of staying with an unfulfilling job for a steady paycheck and a dental plan would kill my soul, so I'll take the excitement of the roller coaster ride any day!"

Gail's best experience, like her worst, is one she lives every day. "It's combining world-travel adventures and the discovery of other cultures with working from my purple home office," she says. "Making a difference while making a living as a playful professional doing what I love and what comes naturally. Inspiring and encouraging others to practice safe stress and energize their lives. Having the freedom to create a terrific lifestyle, follow my calling, and to balance my life as I see fit."

This seems to be the attitude of all the seminar professionals who so generously helped with this book—the joy in a job well done and the desire to make a difference for others. If you go into this business with the right stuff—a willingness to work hard and to learn everything you can, the confidence to promote yourself and your business, and the drive to succeed—chances are you'll do well.

Appendix
Seminar Production Resources

They say you can never be too rich or too thin. While these could be argued, we say, "You can never have enough resources." Therefore, we present for your consideration a wealth of sources for you to check into, check out, and harness for your own personal information blitz.

These sources are tidbits, ideas to get you started on your research. They are by no means the only sources out there, and they should not be taken as the Ultimate Answer. We've done our research, but businesses—like people—tend to move, change, fold, and expand. As we've repeatedly stressed, do your homework. Get out and get investigating.

As an additional push to get you going, we strongly suggest the following: If you haven't yet joined the internet age, do it! Surfing the net is like waltzing through the fabled Library at Alexandria, updated for the millennium, with a breathtaking array of resources literally at your fingertips.

Associations

American Society for Training and Development
1640 King St., Box 1443
Alexandria, VA 22313-2043
(703) 683-8100
www.astd.org

▲

The Direct Marketing Association
1120 Avenue of the Americas
New York, NY 10036-6700
(212) 768-7277
www.the-dma.org

International Association of Speakers Bureaus
2780 Waterfront Pkwy., East Dr., #120
Indianapolis, IN 46214
(317) 297-0872
www.igab.org

International Society of Meeting Planners
1224 N. Nokomis NE
Alexandria, MN 56308
(320) 763-4919
www.iami.org/ismp

International Special Events Society
401 N. Michigan Ave.
Chicago, IL 60611-4267
(800) 688-4737
(312) 321-6853
www.ises.com

Mailing & Fulfillment Service Association
1421 Prince St., #410
Alexandria, VA 22314-2806
(703) 836-9200
www.mfsanet.org

Meeting Professionals International
4455 LBJ Fwy., #1200
Dallas, TX 75244-5903
(972) 702-3000
www.mpiweb.org

National Mail Order Association
2807 Polk St. NE
Minneapolis, MN 55418-2954
(612) 788-4197
for product marketing and development, (612) 788-1673
www.nmoa.org

National Speakers Association
1500 S. Priest Dr.
Tempe, AZ 85281
(480) 968-2552
www.nsaspeaker.org

Book Printers

ANRO Inc.
222 Lancaster Ave., P.O. Box 600
Devon, PA 19333-0600
(800) 355-2676
(610) 687-1200
www.anroinc.com

Thompson-Shore Inc.
7300 W. Joy Rd.
Dexter, MI 48130
(734) 426-3939
www.tshore.com

Books

Entrepreneur's Start Your Own Mail-Order Business, (Entrepreneur Press)

How to Make it Big in the Seminar Business, by Paul Karasik (McGraw-Hill)

Money Talks: How to Make a Million as a Speaker, by Alan Weiss (McGraw-Hill)

Become a Recognized Authority in Your Field in 60 Days or Less!, by Robert W. Bly (Alpha)

Government Agencies

Bureau of the Census
www.census.gov

Federal Trade Commission
www.ftc.gov (Locate a regional office near you on the FTC's web site.)

U.S. Patent and Trademark Office
www.uspto.gov

U.S. Postal Service
www.usps.com

▲

Note: Ask your local bulk-mail processing center—which you can locate by calling your local post office—for copies of Publication 95, Quick Service Guide and the Mailers Companion

Magazines and Publications

Catalog Age
Cowles Business Media
11 River Bend Drive S., Box 4242
Stamford, CT 06907-0242
www.catalogagemag.com

Professional Speaker
National Speakers Association
1500 S. Priest Dr.
Tempe, AZ 85281
(480) 968-2552
www.nsaspeaker.com

Successful Meetings
www.successmtgs.com

Target Marketing
401 N. Broad St.
Philadelphia, PA 19108
www.targetonline.com

Training
50 S. Ninth St.
Minneapolis, MN 55402
(800) 328-4329
(612) 333-0471
www.trainingmag.com

T+D Magazine
American Society for Training and Development
1640 King St., Box 1443
Alexandria, VA 22313-2043
(703) 683-8100,
www.astd.org

Note: Most magazines will send a sample issue free of charge if you call and ask. So do it!

Note: Check into any issue of magazines like *Catalog Age* or *Target Marketing*—advertisements for list brokers, managers, and owners abound.

Mailing List Brokers

Allmedia Inc.
Two Legacy Town Center
6900 Dallas Pkwy., #750
Plano, TX 75024-3537
(469) 467-9100
www.allmediainc.com

American List Counsel
4300 Route 1, CN-5219
Princeton, NJ 08543
(800) ALC-LIST
www.amlist.com

infoUSA
6711 S. 86th Cir., P.O. Box 27347
Omaha, NE 69127-0347
(800) 321-0869
(402) 930-3500
www.infousa.com

Mail Order Software

CMS Solo
NewHaven Software
P.O. Box 3456
Redmond, WA 98073-3456
(425) 458-4670
www.newhavensoftware.com

Mailer's+4
Melissa Data
22382 Avenida Empressa
Rancho Santa Margarita
CA 92688-2112
(800) 635-4772
(949) 589-5200
www.melissadata.com

Mailware Home Office
Core Technologies
4801 Riverbend Rd.

Boulder, CO 80301
(866) 624-5927
www.mailware.com
Note: Most software vendors will send you a free or nominally priced demo if you ask.
So do it!

Merchant Card Services

1st American Card Service.com
P.O. Box 730
Murrieta, CA 92564
(800) 438-8262
(909) 699-9555
www.w.1stamericancardservice.com

Merchant Express
20A Northwest Blvd., #102
Nashua, NH 03063
(888) 845-9457
(603) 429-4300
www.merchantexpress.com

Speakers Bureaus

The All-Star Agency
4829 Powell Rd.
Fairfax, VA 22032
(800) 736-0031
www.allstaragency.com

Golden Gate International Speakers Bureau
42-335 Washington St., #369
Palm Desert, CA 92211
(760) 345-2061
www.ggisb.com

Great Speakers!
359 N. Oak St.
Ukiah, CA 95482
(707) 463-1081
www.greatspeakers.com

Speakers Platform Bureau
699 Mississippi St., #108
San Francisco, CA 94107
www.speaking.com

Speaker Services
4023 Meier St.
Los Angeles, CA 90066
(877) 773-2800 or (310) 822-4922
www.speakerservices.com

Successful Seminar Business Owners

Nance Cheifetz
Sense of Delight
(415) 883-1465
www.senseofdelight.com

Denise Dudley
SkillPath Seminars
P.O. Box 2768
Mission, KS 66201-2768
(800) 873-7545
www.skillpath.com

Gail Hahn, MA, CSP, CPRP
Fun*cilitators
11407 Orchard Green Ct.
Reston, VA 20190
(866) FUN-AT-WORK
www.funcilitators.com

Jerry L. Old, M.D.
13813 W. 57th St.
Shawnee, KS 66216
(913) 962-5399

Larry T. Smith, CSP
National Electrical Seminars
P.O. Box 45408
Omaha, NE 68145-0408
(402) 895-4402
www.electricode.com

Web Conferencing Services

Genesys Conferencing
9139 S. Ridgeline Blvd.
Highlands Ranch, CO 80129
(866) 436-3797 (sales)
www.genesys.com

Microsoft Live Meeting
PlaceWare Inc.
295 N. Bernardo Ave.
Mountain View, CA 94043
(866) 463-3866 (sales)
(650) 526-6100
www.placeware.com

WebEx Communications Inc.
307 W. Tasman Dr.
San Jose, CA 95134
(877) 509-3239
(408) 435-7048 (sales)
www.webex.com

Web Site Solutions (Hosting and Design)

Affinity Internet
www.affinity.com

Earthlink
www.earthlink.net

Homestead Technologies
www.homestead.com

Interland
www.interland.com

Verio
www.verio.com

Glossary

Additional profit center: another method of earning money from customers, e.g., selling back-of-the-room products.

Back-of-the-room products: products such as books, audiotapes, and videotapes sold by seminar professionals.

BOR products: see *back-of-the-room products.*

Breakout session: a seminar held at the same time as several other seminars during the course of a convention.

Bulk mail: mail sent at discounted prices following special postal guidelines.

Buyer list: see *response list.*

CEU: see continuing education unit.

Chargeback: customer return or dispute of merchandise paid by credit card.

Compiled list: mailing list composed of people in specific categories, e.g., doctors, lawyers, Manhattan residents.

Concurrent session: see *breakout session.*

Conference: group get-together, usually lasting a few days to a week, designed by associations, corporations, or other organizations for their members.

Contact sheet: one-page seminar description.

Content sheet: see *contact sheet*.

Continuing education unit: measure of continuing education credits required by professional organizations.

Convention: see *conference*.

Direct marketing: another term for mail order; any form of shop-at-home-or-office order placement from mail or telephone to fax or e-mail.

Facilitator: a seminar professional who assists participants in learning intangibles like self-confidence, motivation, or creativity.

Float: overage on hotel seating and pre-ordered food and beverages.

Focus group: a group of people gathered for the purpose of conducting market research.

Fulfillment: a mail order term for the practice of getting an ordered item from seller to buyer.

General session presentation: a presentation in which the entire convention population constitutes the audience.

High-concept: a Hollywood term meaning a script idea that gets its point across in a few short words. See *program manager*.

Inclusive fee: prearranged fee paid to presenter for travel expenses rather than payment of exact travel costs.

ISBN: International Standard Book Number, required for cataloging by libraries, booksellers, and distributors.

Keynote speech: a speech that highlights a feature of a conference, like an after-dinner speech or one that opens the meeting.

Letter shop: a company that processes direct-mail pieces—inserts, folds, staples, sorts, and stamps.

List broker: a company specializing in mailing-list rentals.

Mailing list: a group of names and addresses used by direct marketers.

Mail Order or Telephone Rule: the Federal Trade Commission ruling that regulates direct-marketing businesses.

Meeting: see *conference*.

Per diem: a daily allowance paid to traveling seminar presenters to cover meals, taxis, tips, and other sundries.

Perfect binding: a method of binding paperback books.

Premium: a mail order term for an item given free when a more expensive item, such as a seminar enrollment, is purchased.

Presentation kit: see *promo kit*.

Presenter: a seminar professional who gives a speech, training session or other seminar program.

Private seminar: one that's sponsored by a corporation or organization and is open only to members of that group.

Pro bono: professional service offered at no charge to a deserving group or individual.

Program manager: greets seminar participants, hands out name tags and workbooks, collects enrollment fees, and answers general questions.

Promo or promotional kit: a packet of promotional materials sent to prospective clients.

Psychographics: a method of determining customers by psychological profile.

Public seminar: one given by the seminar professional and open to anyone who pays the ticket price.

Qualified buyer: a customer who has already purchased products or services by mail order.

Response list: a mailing list composed of people who have previously responded to specific mail order campaigns, e.g., people who enroll in gardening seminars or companies that enroll their employees in training programs.

RFM: a mailing list formula meaning recency, frequency, and money.

Salting: the practice of inserting fictitious names and addresses into a mailing list so that the company renting the list to others can tell if it has been used illegally.

Select: a specific category of mailing list names based on age, geographic region or income bracket.

Seminar: a program designed to give attendees information on a particular topic.

Seminar assistant: see program manager.

Speaker: a seminar professional who gives talks or speeches before an audience.

Speech: a talk given by a speaker before a group, usually lasting from 30 minutes to two hours.

Standard mail: see *bulk mail*.

Trainer: a seminar professional who teaches small groups of people specific skills.

Training program: see *workshop*.

Vanity publisher: a publishing house that prints books for a flat fee and pays no advances or royalties to the writer.

Webinar: a seminar given on the internet.

Workshop: a seminar in which attendees become participants through hands-on activities.

Index